On the Cover:

"Humans have a great capacity to love, animals have a great capacity to forgive. Humans can join together for something they love and miracles happen. I am an example of this. All too often humans think that to love too much shows weakness when in reality it shows great strength."

~ Kazuma

Testimonials

As a publisher with a specialty in medical journals, I approach any unorthodox practice with skepticism. Imagine my reaction to an animal communicator. Only after I had experienced several instances of valid, unassailable incidents ranging from detection of medical conditions (thyroid and infection) to my own animals' behavior modifications, did I become a firm believer. Debbie and Sue have convinced me that there are communication skills far beyond the norm. I appreciate knowing that. You will too.

Charles Hunt

We must listen to the animals and understand their lessons, for if we do not, their voices will eventually go silent. I have always communicated with animals on their terms. Debbie goes deeper, it is a gift and it is her job to make sure their voices are heard. Untamed Voices provides readers with a voice that can't be ignored, one that must be heard and if you choose to listen with your heart and feel their presence, you will begin to understand them as individuals.

Wilbur McCauley
Animal Behaviorist

Enchanted first hand knowledge

As one of the original Volunteers with Tigers For Tomorrow in Fort Piece, FL., I have had the unique opportunity to watch the growth, development and evolution of the non-profit Exotic Animal Rescue and Preserve that Susan Steffens started years ago. Others see it as what it is, I see it as where it has come from and where it is going. To be deeply involved with Susan Steffens and her incredible love and understanding of animals has left me with an impression that will last for life.

Daniel Phil Gray, Jr.

Debbie has successfully helped me with many issues with my animals. From helping with the hardest decision to help a friend pass, to the simplest of what's "up." To be able to give my animals the respect and right to choose when the battle for life exceeds the quality of life is invaluable. To hear their last words, and receive their last message, makes an awful moment have deep meaning. Her talent is matched with honesty, integrity, and a sense of humor.

Dr. Anne Crawshaw

If you listen… they will speak.

What they say…. is sure to surprise, enlighten, and open our hearts in ways you never thought possible. Sue Steffens, owner of Tigers for Tomorrow Exotic Animal Preserve, and Debbie McGillivray, a Professional Animal Communicator, combine forces to give the animals a voice. This book will allow you to look into the spirit of these magnificent beings and share with you direct messages from the animals while uncovering their wisdom, depth of emotion, intelligence, and psychic awareness.

Sue Steffens   and   Debbie McGillivray

About the Authors:

Sue Steffens is founder and executive director of Tigers For Tomorrow Exotic Animal Preserve, Inc., a 140 acre Wild Animal Preserve and Rescue for animals that have lost their jobs or owners. Tigers For Tomorrow is a last stop for all the animals that come to live at the preserve. All animals are equally respected and given their dignity.

"Each animal at the preserve is considered an individual with unique personalities, emotions, likes, and dislikes. Caretakers provide the highest quality of care during the entire life of each animal and provide them with reverence when their time comes to move on to the spirit world. It is our hope that when you close this book you will no longer see each of these animals as *what* they are, but you will understand fully *who* they are."

-Sue Steffens.

"When we animals come here, we are suddenly dignified and important. We are no longer throw-aways. We become the cell, the organs and the oxygen in a world where we are the focus. It is truly a world of our own, where we are the masters."

- Benny the Black Leopard.

Debbie McGillivray is a professional animal communicator and pet intuitive with over 15 years experience and clients across the globe. She is author of the book *"The Complete Idiot's Guide to Pet Psychic Communication"* and has been featured on the National Geographic Channel as well as many local news programs. She believes that we all hold the ability to communicate with our animal friends and is dedicated to opening people's hearts and minds to this phenomenon. She holds workshops nationally to help people develop this ability. You can find out more about Debbie and her work at www.Animaltelepathy.com.

"I feel very blessed to be able to bridge the gap between humans and animals, to bring about healing, understanding, and growth. It is through this subtle communication that questions are answered, compromise is achieved and harmony restored. Animals have so much to teach us, all we have to do is open our hearts and listen. It is my goal and vision for people and animals to understand each other on a deeper level through mutual respect, communication, and compassion, so that we may once again live in harmony with all living things. Only then will this world be truly healed."

- Debbie McGillivray.

Untamed Voices

If you listen…they will speak

"Silent Voices don't always fall on deaf ears; you are here to share our story."

Debbie McGillivray and Sue Steffens

For more information please visit us online at:
www.untamedvoices.com

Untamed Voices
Copyright © 2012 by Debbie McGillivray and Sue Steffens

ISBN: 1495450163
ISBN 13: 978 - 1495450167

CONTENTS

CONTENTS

This book is dedicated to all animals both alive and in spirit that have touched the souls of humans through their joy, grace, forgiveness, and love.

May we all learn to live with an Untamed Heart.

For more information about the animals featured here, please visit us online at:

www.untamedvoices.com

Foreword
By Sue Steffens

I feel very blessed to have realized my passion at such a young age. So many people are never able to find what they love in life let alone be lucky enough to be able to pursue it as a career. I never wake up hating my job; tired - yes, exhausted - sometimes, but never do I dread going to work. I don't have to fight traffic or worry about the latest fashions.

My world revolves around the animals. I grew up loving animals but never did I imagine such a life as to be surrounded by some of God's most magnificent species of apex predators every day. It really gives you a good perspective of "not sweating the small stuff."

I did not grow up wanting to own a tiger but for as long as I can remember, animals have been part of my life. I don't think my life would make much sense without them. I also grew up talking to animals. Being the youngest of three girls, with six and nine years between us, I didn't have playmates, I had play-pets. Things haven't changed much since I was a child. My mother used to tell me that animals don't talk, and as an adult she now believes me but often reminds me not to tell people that I talk to animals. She says that they may come lock me up thinking I'm crazy. It's the same thing many of my friends and acquaintances have said to me over the years when I would urge them to call Debbie to help look for a lost pet or to help with saying a final good-bye.

I don't believe in coincidences, I believe EVERYTHING happens just as it is supposed to. I was lucky enough to meet Debbie ten years ago when a communicator I had used was unavailable. I had just gotten the preserve started in Fort Pierce, Florida. Meeting Debbie was a blessing and a great opportunity to explore any questions I had about animal communication.

Debbie has taught many workshops at my preserve over the years and assisted me in rescues, relocations, health issues, and in saying goodbye to many of my good friends and family members. During her first workshop in Florida, my big Alfa-Male timber wolf, Bear, explained to her that he was with me to teach me about death. He explained to her that I took the loss of an animal too personally, that there was more to it than I was yet aware of and that I would soon learn.

I used to fear losing one of my animals. I no longer do this. It is still hard; I still cry, sometimes two or three years after an animal has passed, because I still miss them when I think of them, but my losses do not cut me as deep as they did before. Not because I care less, but because I now have a better understanding that we are all connected in body and in spirit.

With the help of my good friend Debbie McGillivray, combined with my knowledge of animal behavior, we are able to give the animals at Untamed Mountain what they need emotionally and physically. We are able to give each and every animal a rich and fulfilling life. Many of the relationships I see among other human beings are not as deep as the relationships that I see my staff establish with these animals whose voices are soon to be heard.

It is my wish that, as you embark on this journey with Debbie and me, you will not only fall in love with the animals whose voices are untamed, but will be able to keep an open mind and understand that the animals are here to help heal our planet and act as guides. "Animals are masters of forgiveness," my husband, Wilbur McCauley reminds me. There is so much we can learn from the animals if we listen.

~ Sue Steffens
Founder and Executive Director
Tigers For Tomorrow Exotic Animal Preserve

Introduction

by Debbie McGillivray

If you listen... they will speak

For as long as I can remember I have had a deep love of animals. I was a very shy child and this created uneasy social interactions. School was excruciating and I found solace being around animals. They were healing to me. At family gatherings I would sit in the corner with the cat and my shyness would vanish for the moment. I was teased a lot as a kid. Sometimes it was because I was shy, other times because I loved animals so much, and sometimes because I was just an awkward kid. That didn't help my self esteem much, to say the least. But the animals never seemed to notice. They didn't care what I looked like, and they made me feel special.

I knew at a very early age I wanted to work with animals. They helped me and I wanted to help them. I always had a love of horses and wanted to be around them from dawn to dusk. I can still remember being about ten years old sitting in a little Shetland Pony's stall for hours just waiting for him to talk to me. I thought that if I waited long enough he would talk. If I only knew then what I know now! He was probably saying, "Beat it kid, you're annoying me!"

They did finally talk to me, but not till many years later. I will never forget my first "validated" communication with an animal. It was at Spring Farm Cares Animal Sanctuary in upstate New York. I was taking an introductory course on how to communicate with the animals through telepathy. I was admittedly a skeptic and didn't have a telepathic bone in my body as far as I was concerned. But after two days of exercises I finally got the validation I so desperately needed in order to believe that what I had experienced with the animals for years was more than just empathy, it was communication.

I remember that day as if it were yesterday. That was the day I found my path, thanks to a handsome little goat named Tyler. I walked into the barn on the final morning of the workshop. I was drawn to a goat that was perched upon his gate cocking his head to one side eyeing me. I walked over to him, notebook in hand. I heard him say through my mind, "Don't you think I'm handsome?" I answered him in my mind, "well, yes." Ugh, I rolled my eyes thinking to myself, my husband is going to think I am nuts. Then I heard, "your pants are funny" as he nipped at the fabric. (He was right; I was wearing flowered stretch pants - a fashion no-no).

What came next made me stop thinking it was my imagination. "What do you think of my ornaments?" I was taken aback because I knew I hadn't made that up. "Move along now, others need to speak with me," he finished. And off I went, a bit confused about what had just happened. Later that day, talking to the teacher about my interaction with Tyler the goat, she validated the fact that each morning the staff asks Tyler what he has for "ornaments." It is an ongoing joke there because he manages to have all kinds of things hang off his horns. But at the time I was talking to him, he was ornament free! I was floored! That was the validation I needed ... I was off and running. I read every book I could on the subject, took classes and practiced every chance I could get. Years later I took my knowledge to the professional level knowing it was my purpose to bridge the gap between the human and animal world through communication and compassion.

That was over seventeen years ago. I am happy to say I am still learning from these spiritual beings. I am humbled by the scope of their love and understanding on so many levels.

We need to be their voice now so that more people can understand the wisdom of these great beings. Many of us go through life with tunnel vision. The animals are asking us to step out of our time capsule, to get our heads out of our minds, to plug into our hearts and to make changes so that this great planet and all the beings who inhabit it can live in harmony.

With this world changing at a rapid pace we cannot rely on the human logic alone to make the necessary changes the world needs. We need wisdom from all sources. The animals have always been tuned into energies we cannot see or understand and to the changes in the environment.

Many animals are sent here with the divine purpose of helping the human species to grow and evolve. They reignite what many have lost in the quest for abundant material things and not things of the heart. They are sent here to re-connect us with the earth and our spirit.

Humans, as intelligent as we are, can get easily lost on the roads of the masses, losing the true value of our existence. Many animals feel it is their purpose to help save humanity and this earth before too much damage is done. It is our goal to help bridge the gap of understanding between humans and the animal kingdom so that harmony can one day be restored so that all living things will be treated with dignity and respect.

~ Debbie McGillivray
Animal Communicator

Debbie and Ayla

I first began communicating with "Big Cats" when I met Sue Steffens at the Tigers for Tomorrow Preserve when it was located in Fort Pierce, Florida. She had called me to work with a few of the animals there, including wolves, tortoises and of course, Tigers. I was used to working with domestic animals so working with Tigers in person was a new experience for me. Blake was the first Tiger I was blessed to work with and he was eager and willing. He settled my fears as he chuffed along the fence to me and the minute I relaxed enough, he began communicating. I was honored to be able to communicate with such a magnificent being. There is something special about being around these large cats that sticks to your soul in an awe inspiring way.

Communication

This book is a compilation of conversations and connections with various animals in different locations. Some animals were wild, some held in captivity, and others domesticated. As you read their stories, let the messages flow into your heart and tickle your soul.

It is our goal to help the animals verbalize their messages for humanity at this crucial time for our planet. This is a time when change is happening rapidly and it is important that humans become more spiritually aware of why we are here. We feel honored to be able to bring these messages to you and hope that you will find it in your hearts to look at animals in a new light with awareness and respect. They are our kindred souls.

Next time you go to an animal sanctuary, wildlife preserve, or even a zoo, understand that each animal you see has a personality, a purpose, and a wide range of opinions, thoughts and emotions. There is an interwoven society among the animals in these places that most people never get to see or understand.

Many sanctuaries and preserves, as well as some zoos and breeders, make sure that the animals in their care are happy and healthy. We toured a few of these places during the development of this book. Many of those animals are featured here. This book is part one in a series. In the second book we will expand focus to breeding facilities, rehabilitation centers, and wild animals. Through the words of the animals, we hope to fight extinction so that generations to come may admire the stripes of a tiger, hear the roar of a lion, and marvel at the communication between a pack of wolves.

Animals help the human race grow. Their communication with us serves an important purpose. Animals do not judge, condemn, or hate. They do give advice where and when it is needed. They share their love with us, because they see God in all of us.

Despite the damage we have done to the earth, ocean and skies, animals stand beside us and help us grow. Their plea is that we reclaim our connection to the earth and nurture her because it is us who have hurt her.

When we start to heal the earth and all its creatures, we will heal ourselves. When we live in a world where all life matters and is equal, we will have true balance.

The world is not ours. We borrow it for a short time. During this time we must learn to live in harmony with all living things while we are here.

Open your hearts and feel the love that comes from every living thing. Feel your soul come alive. Start each day by giving thanks and becoming aware. Then take notice, for your life will change.

Love is the strongest of emotions. Most of us have not fully opened our heart to love's limitless potential. We fear hurt or pain. It is important to learn how to love without boundaries, to love without expectations, and to love fearlessly. We should try to walk on the path of heart and conscience, not on the path of greed and self-superiority. The animals can teach us this.

Animal Communication De-Mystified

Animal Communication is the ability to understand an animal on a deeper level through the use of telepathy. Telepathy is the direct transmission of feelings, thoughts, mental images, emotions, and sensations. The more we are aware of this mode of communication the more receptive we become. Animals relate to each other through verbal, physical, and telepathic communication. Humans can also use each of these vehicles to communicate with their animal friends. Through verbal and physical communication we can get our animals to understand what we want them to do by teaching them certain commands through repetition and positive feedback. However, it is telepathic communication that will allow us to understand what makes the animal tick. Telepathic communication allows us to "talk" to the animals, and see and hear what they say back. It connects mind to mind and heart to heart. It is immediate and direct. Amazing! Plus, we can all do it. We are all born with the ability to communicate through telepathy. Socialization, however, has taught us to rely on verbal communication and our telepathic abilities become stagnant. Like any new language you learn, unless used regularly it becomes harder to do. Animal Communication is a valuable tool that many people use to help them understand their animals and the animal world on a deeper level. It is the key to unlock all the untold wonders of the animal kingdom.

**When the logical mind and the intuitive mind can work together,
greater spiritual awakening is achieved.**

This book is a compilation of the messages provided from some of the world's most exotic species right down to man's best friend. You may be surprised, enlightened and saddened by what they have to share.

It is time to give the animals a voice. They know more about this world and our species than you may think. Open your heart and prepare to view the world with new eyes and a new understanding of the world around you and the animals who are more than just flesh
and blood, but messengers from God.

What do the animals need to tell us?

Where do they go when they die?

Can animals sense world changes and disaster?

What advice do they have for us?

Turn the page and find out............

Benny

"I want people to know that we are all different. Please do not link us all into the same category just because we are of one species. Just like humans, we have different experiences and souls. Most people just look and observe. Only a few ever really "talk" to us and ask us what we are about, why we are here. This is where we will start. My story is simple – it is about me and a girl and a vision that merged into one. We saw a world created to dignify the throwaways. How can some of the mightiest and rarest beasts on earth be treated with such malice and disrespect. This is where our story starts."

Benny lives at the Tigers For Tomorrow Exotic Animal Preserve on Untamed Mountain in Alabama. Benny refers to himself as 'the Magician', and if you spend any time with him you are sure to find out why. He helped orchestrate this book in many ways. Benny is confident, stunning, witty, humorous and magical. I am always humbled by his presence.

Benny – Black Leopard

"When the animals come here, they are suddenly dignified and important. They are no longer throwaways, they become the cell, the organs and the oxygen in a world where we are the focus. It is truly a world of our own, where we are the masters.

"When we eat the flesh of another being it is just that. We are not eating your soul or your essence or your personality, no it is just flesh. In a hunt, the predator can sometimes see the soul of our prey leave the body before the body dies. In a way, we are allowing the soul to fly.

"In order to create a new tomorrow, people need to feel their souls again and experience the heartbeat of life. They need to know the ties that unite us all. Do people understand that treating just one being with disrespect and hate creates a blemish and a hole in the soul of existence? That cannot be undone. Love is the true source of life and joy.

"People are very visual as you know. If they were able to travel to different realms, like I can do, they would quickly realize what they are missing. Things take on a new vibrancy when one travels in an energetic state. What does this mean? It means that when you are one with something, you not only see it, but you embody it. You see, feel, taste, and smell it. If I want to know more about something, I become it, in my mind. All of my cells and senses think it is real, so I truly 'become' it. I have sensed humans beyond their knowledge. I have tasted the salty sweat on their skin, felt the scarce hair on his limbs, and noticed the lack of smell and taste they had. Truly I could not wait to get out of human body back into my cat body. Humans, I notice, are so controlled by the logic of their brain that they operate much differently than we do. I think I can help people see more clearly and feel less lost.

"It is as if they wear many covers, layer upon layer. Underneath all of them is their soul, their true self. I just want them to walk naked, to feel what it is to be free from all layers, diversions, walls, and masks. In this humble state, they will feel like never before. Yes, your species needs to 'feel' once again. You are so linear you need to start feeling on all levels. Then you will be in tune once again to all that was lost so long ago."

"I am here to help. But I will not always be kind, because I tell it like it is. We don't have time to take it slow. I want your species to wake up. We can tell you how to do it. Sometimes through shock and sometimes through awe, but always, through the heart.

"I do not call myself the king here. I leave that to those who are more suited visually. I am the heart and soul of this place. You could say I was part of the seed that was planted to help Sue and I create "this" refuge. There is a delicate balance of intricate emotions and souls intertwined throughout here. That is what I watch over. The overall vision is to stay pure and true to the purpose here. I am like the magician. I'm a wise, magical, and a reluctant hero of sorts in an unseen world. I oversee all that is here. All of us have a purpose here, even you. Stop and listen. We all make up a live beating heart. We fill this place with a beat all of its own. When you are here, you become part of that beat, but only if you are worthy. Many people come and go here, but only a few experience this rhythm of life.

"I can shift between realms. One of the things I have learned is that the higher your vibration, the more you can manifest. You will also attract to yourself things of a similar vibration. There are many animals in spirit here, and they tell me that they can create anything they think about when in spirit form. It is a bit harder to do that here, but not impossible. In spirit, everything has a higher vibration so manifesting a perfect world is easy. But here we must maintain a higher vibration for longer periods of time. By surrounding ourselves with beings of a higher vibration, it is a little easier."

So how do you raise your vibration?

"It is quite simple. Act only out of love. The more often you do this, the higher the vibration."

If you could manifest anything, would you ever manifest yourself being in the wild and living free?

"I do manifest, and I did manifest what you see here. I do not know the wild, and I would not put myself there. It would not serve my purpose at this time. I am provided for and loved. I am working on a purpose larger than myself and this is where I need to be. I have manifested things perfectly. Besides, the meals here are outstanding. I get whatever I want. This is a sacred place, and the beings here are special. We are a collaborative, energetic force, and I am proud to be one of the facilitators of it."

Do you have anything else you want to share with me?

"Silent voices – don't always fall on deaf ears. You are here to share our story."

Roxy

"When a heart has loved fully without restraint, you will have witnessed what it feels like for a dog to love. We do not hold back. When we love something we love it with our whole being."

Sue and Roxy

Some animals are such wise souls with knowledge of lifetimes that they humble those who listen. I asked Roxy what she had to share with me and all I needed to do was tune in and listen. What some of these spiritual beings share is truly amazing once you fully digest it all. When I sit down and read back my notes from many of these sessions I am moved to tears, filled with joy, or armed with information to help us all evolve. When working with Roxy, the information streamed through like a clear radio channel, smooth and uninterrupted. She has the energy like that of a grandmother, kind, nurturing and all knowing. She is a wise old soul.

Roxy – Golden Retriever

"I would like to talk about the mother energy that many dogs have. It is a natural nurturing that comes from within and above. Our deepest desire is to partner with people, to love them, protect them and have them acknowledge this back. I call it the mother energy because that is what it is. We come to earth with the ability to exhibit unconditional love. Forgiveness is not something we think about, it just happens.

"I have witnessed firsthand the circle of life many times here. Living with a lot of animals really puts it in front of you more often than not. There is always a flow that happens when a soul leaves this earth plane. When the energy leaves, it is like a wave or a windswept burst. What everyone must know is that we can see this energy leave. It is visual to us. We also know that as the energy leaves, it has to be replaced. That is just a fact. So we always know something will come because there can never be just a void. When energy is removed, more comes in. Sometimes it will be another animal, maybe a person or friend for a short time. A bird may appear for longer than normal in your yard, a new flower may bloom, but some type of energy will appear. This energy may be there for a reason, or just to hold the spot until another comes in. It is a constant movement of energy.

"I really enjoy when we have babies come join us here. There is an energy a baby brings that is like no other. There is excitement, innocence, and pure mayhem at times. I love the enthusiasm the younger animals bring, and I relish in the wisdom of the long-timers. There is an inner society that goes on when multiple animals share the same section of space. This is not just canine but across all species that I have witnessed. And within this society are rules within smaller groups. Overseeing all are the masters. The masters are those that earn the title either through respect from the other animals, divine wisdom, and sometimes age and experience. We have many masters here. For those that are at the master level, there is no competition. If there is jealously and competition, the animal is not ready to be a master. There are a few here who are very anxious to be considered masters, but have too much ego to advance to this level. I smile as I say this.

"Energy and intention are not hidden from animals. That is why our society runs well. The beings who are masters have earned it. You probably have a society within your own animals as well. It is when the humans get too involved in this that it becomes disruptive to the flow of the animal society. Some things must be worked out as nature intended. The people who live and care for animals on a deep level begin to think the way we do. They understand things from our viewpoint and when this happens they become a master on the human level. There are animal and human "masters" who rise above ego for the higher purpose of all. I have been blessed to witness many in my life. There are also some who fall from grace, but I will not expound on those. They are life lessons that must be dealt with quickly and efficiently.

"Masters stabilize a society. They are beacons for the light, beacons of truth, justice, and authority. They operate in the physical, mental, and spiritual level. They have a higher purpose than self.

"Below the masters are the nurturers. We are the ones who bring up the young and who counsel and love unconditionally. We are the heart of the society.

"We have the protectors who guard the property on all levels, both the energetic and the physical. They also anchor and ground the energy in a spiritual way.

"We have the reporters. These animals work with the masters to keep them informed of any change happening within the property or with the animals. They are also very good at alerting their groups of anything that needs to be broadcasted.

"We have the healers. These animals come here to heal themselves, and then go on to heal others.

"We have the ambassadors who range in personality from clowns to being attention-getters and who must work well with humans. That is their purpose, to bridge the gap into the human mind and heart to facilitate change. Then we have the apprentices who will eventually fall into one of these roles.

"This is the structure of the society within the sanctuary as I know it. We have many other things that go on, but for the sake of keeping it simple, I will leave it as such."

"People must know that the heart (love center) never dies. The heart (love) is the soul. They are not separate things. I go through life each day honoring the ability my heart has to love all that is around me. I appreciate every moment. I do my best everyday and I do not look back regretting, because I do my best. I do not look to the future and want for anything. I stay in the present. In this state of mind, I can be the best I can be at all times. A mind spent in the past or in the future is of no use here. It is what we think and do in the present that matters. The future comes out of this.

"When a heart has loved fully without restraint you will have witnessed what it feels like for a dog to love. We do not hold back. When we love something we love it with our whole being. There is no mid way, or kind of. There is no 'like', we either love or we don't. We are born this way. This is the vibration of dog. We are made up of fur, bones, tails and love. We put on a display for you of pure joy and the raw energy of love.

"Humans are an explicit gift with the rare challenge of having too much information in a fast moving world. They can be at odds with their inner truth and risk losing their connection to the soul. They are the makers and breakers of all that we have. We have reason to fear those that lose their connection to the soul which connects us all. However, every lost soul can be found, and that is where we come in. The animal world operates behind the scenes. Silently we tug at people to get back on track. This is done in a variety of ways as you can imagine. I operate out of love. My goal at this time is to age gracefully with a heart bursting at the seams with love."

Roxy does not give up. Sue was told that Roxy came from a puppy mill and was purchased on a whim. Her owner frequently drank too much, was very loud and kept her locked in a crate most of the time. Roxy had severe social disorders when she came to live with Sue, and over the many years together they have both faced their fears and have experienced an amazing ride together. She has helped Sue raise many baby tigers and lions in addition to many other rescued animals. Roxy ruled fairly, but with a fierce power. In her younger years she disciplined and scorned many youngsters when they acted inappropriately. She is a wonderful role model for all humans and animals. Sue says, "As I grow old, I hope to have the grace and dignity that she so proudly displays despite the disabilities of age. I tell her all the time that I hope she comes back into a human body some day to take care of me when I am old."

Furry

"It is our sacrifice and our sorrow that will hopefully bring humans into the knowing once again. I will always stand tall and full of might, because I know truly who I am. I am part of the beating heart of earth. I have a right to be here."

Furry Lion lives at the Tigers for Tomorrow Wild Animal Preserve along with many of the other animals featured here. He commands great respect from all. Lions bond strongly with those within their pride, and many times they consider one of their caretakers a part of their pride. Furry's person is Wilbur, who he respectfully adores. They have a bond that goes far beyond person and animal, it is one that exists at the soul level.

Furry – Lion

Is there anything you would like people to know?

"I stand for Conviction of Character. I think people need to learn to stand on both feet and stick by their truth. They need to know who they are, what is their truth and why. Many wobble on one small piece of truth, losing sight of who they are and why they are here. It is not until they are forced to take notice – God sits them down and says, Stop, Look, Listen... it is then that they stand firmly once again, they are embodied in truth, in love and respect for themselves and others. Humans can get lost in the realm of selfish thought. They need to see us and the world as one. A human that feels this has a pure heart. When I see a human with this quality I have respect. Many are not like this. They exist in a world of pretence and nonsense. They pay attention to those things that have no weight in the big scheme of things, Love and Life. They seek out that which they think has value, and lose sight of that which really does. Some animals bring out the best in people, and some animals pay the price for those who never see the light."

Lakota

"The moon sings a song, telling us of the day to come. I am grateful for each rise and fall of it."

Lakota – Gray Wolf in Spirit

Lakota is a very wise being. I had the pleasure of knowing her when she was in her physical body. Towards the end of her physical life here, Lakota had a specific message for Sue. She wanted her to know that although her body was very ill, she could not leave until Sue understood that she would be getting three juvenile wolves who would be the divine ones and they were meant to take over her wolf enclosure after she leaves this earth. She also explained that when she was ready to pass into spirit Sue would know because the earth would shake. Once the three wolves had been found, Lakota began to let go of her earthly ties. Sue stayed by Lakota's side during this time and on an overcast day she turned her back to Sue and sent her away. As Lakota lay quietly with her friend Sandy, the sky darkened and hail thundered upon the ground. As the storm raged, Sue kept hearing the words Lakota said over and over. The earth shook and Lakota was gone.

Can you tell me what it is like when you pass into spirit?

"Passing out of a physical body is a surrendering to the great hands of light. When our spirit begins to lift from the body, many try to hold on, but when it is time, there is nothing that can be done except to surrender to this great force. It is powerful and fast, dizzying to some as you shift into a spiritual realm. Then you begin to feel the immense love infused over you, as if you are weak and limp, yet full of a vibration of love, like no other. You are helpless to this power, yet all trusting. You are instantly humbled and infantile, birthing into a new plane of existence. Patient and pure you transition into an incredible brightness. Although the light is bright, it does not hurt your eyes. You feel yourself once again and know that you are no longer in the old body. You have a desire to see more and once you do they all come into view."

What comes into view?

"Whatever or whomever is waiting for you there. Your angels help you from the body. I know this because I have seen their wings. I have felt hands supporting me as I left my physical body. When you get to the light, the faces of those you have known before come into view. It is like a birth. They are excited to see you, yet you feel somehow infantile until you get accustomed to this new world. It is truly glorious, but some take longer than others to comprehend the full extent of where they are and who they are with."

"Sometimes the attachment to the physical plane inhibits the speed of the transition on the 'God' plane. Once we have fully gone through this transition, we understand on a very deep level that which we have learned and taught on a soul level on the earth plane. This is also when we assign ourselves a continuing educational course for the growth of the soul. We move within our soul family so we are always supported with love and with light. The only time we are ever alone is when we have lost the connection with our 'God' love. But we are truly never alone. Once we are in touch with this love we see how connected we all truly are. When you are in spirit this is vitally true. I think the human race should experience being in spirit while still in body. This would be the ultimate quick fix to the physical world. But sadly they forget. Just a minute of time in spirit would be enough to get in touch again with the understanding of divine love and the connection with all. I share my bed with humans and animals here. There is no competition, no hatred. It is the true garden of love. This is our deepest desire for the earth at this time, to re-establish this harmony among all."

Orion, Valhala and Valkeri

"The young species coming in now will be excellent communicators and serve a larger purpose for the good of the planet."

Orion (above), Valhala and Valkeri - Wolves

These are wolves that came to live at Tigers for Tomorrow and reside in Lakota's enclosure.

"We represent a new generation of animals sent here among humans. The young species coming in now will be excellent communicators and serve a larger purpose for the good of the planet. That does not mean all is okay. This is happening because humans do not have enough initiative to make things turn around in time. Even new humans emerging at this time will understand a higher level of being. We call it 'soul consciousness' emerging from the 'higher self'. The 'higher self' will be no longer be detached from ordinary thought and everyday activities. We will operate with the 'higher self' intact decisions will be made based on a higher meaning and outcome. The three of us represent this. We are the trio of the heart, soul, and spirit - the qualities needed in balance for a heaven-like existence."

How is the soul different from the spirit?

"The soul is the body or house for the spirit. The spirit is the energy which the soul projects. The soul is the energetic body, the eternal body for an ever- emerging spirit."

Do you see any visions for the future? Premonitions?
(Valkeri, the white wolf steps forward and speaks.)

"We see a cloud that will appear over the Sun. It will last longer than normal, many weeks. It will not be a time to panic. We must insist upon this. All resources can be obtained from original sources. Be smart. The only way to come out of the dark is to uphold the light. Everyone will be experiencing this reality differently. For some it will seem like forever and for others just a blip in time. It will not faze them. It will turn up the dial on consciousness, group thought and survival. This may create acts of harmony which would mean evolving as a species, or may create disharmony which would be actions based on fear and danger. There are waves of consciousness we feel, but they come and go. They must stay longer. Now is the time."

Can you tell me your purpose here?

Orion: "I anchor the energy. I am the protector and grounder."

Valkeri: "I keep the energy flowing. This flushes out the dark and keeps the light circulating. There is a constant fluctuation and pulsation of energy from all sources."

Valhala: "I am the peacemaker and land worker. I work with the energy of the land. I am a junior worker, there are many others who are masters of this technique. The Native Americans used this to harvest and cultivate the land. By working with the land and mountains, sky and sea, we can stay safe. With our inability to move away from storms and impending danger, we must work with the land to ensure harmonic resolution in the event of an uproar in atmospheric instability."

Valkeri

Valhala

Miss Puss

"We don't filter love, we embrace and give it fully."

Miss Puss - Cougar

"As cats we do not struggle with beauty. We feel it throughout our being. We see so many people come and go here. Some people come many times. I can hear and understand their souls. The noise that comes from inside a person can be very loud. I can see a grown man or woman and instantly see a little child deep inside their being, squatting down with hands on head crying. I can hear the crying, and I can hear what that child is saying. Perhaps this is because the soul is broken, or fragmented. I am not sure. But I can hear the crying and the pleas for help over and over again.

"At first I thought it interesting that other people around did not respond to it. Then I realized that they did not hear it. Not even the person it was coming from could hear their own broken cries for help.

"I can sense those who do not know their true beauty. Beauty is an outward extension of the soul, and when you are in touch with your spirit, your inner light, your purpose, your soul, you exude beauty and you see beauty. Those who are not in touch with this do not see the world as it is. To them, it is monochromatic and negative. Those who are in touch see miracles, colors, and patterns of love and life all around themselves. They see the harmony of life and respond to this with love. They understand the preciousness of life.

"I do not feel sorry for people that are "unaware" or have a broken soul. It makes me distrustful. It's not their fault, but I guess I want them to see what I see so they can fix themselves. They could mend the bridge so that we can all exist on a more harmonious plane. If we all fixed the broken bridges within us that keep us from the divine, access to a higher existence would become immediate, palpable and real. Fix the bridges and all that was lost will be found within you."

What advice do you have for people to accomplish this?

"They need to rescue that part of them that became detached... the part that refuses to move forward; the part that chooses anger, guilt, and resentment as its source of nutrition instead of love. They need to reach out, take the hand of the child inside, and bring it into the light of love and forgiveness.

"I have seen many souls become awakened, just like that. It does not have to be a lengthy process. Many of the animals who have come here have had hopeless lives of being broken and disconnected from who they are. I have seen a dark place deep inside them suddenly become light. Eyes that were cold, distrustful and listless become bright and curious. All it takes is love.

"In order to be able to heal in this way, they must accept love. In order to fully accept love, one must feel worthy. Even just a little bit, and then the magic can happen. I see this often. The gift of love can only be received if the person or animal is willing to receive it.

"Animals love unconditionally; we are direct descendants of God. We don't filter love; we embrace and give it fully. Humans have the problem of filtering emotions, so that the purity may be lost. We are here to help you see this. To help you feel this.

"Love really can heal all. I love the music of life, the symphony one hears when things are in harmony. I love to observe this. I believe I am here for a reason."

Do you ever wish you were in the wild?

"You cannot miss something that you have not fully experienced."

What changes are coming for the human species in the upcoming years?

"It will be a time for your souls to heal, to become one again. I mean, most of you (humans) have such fragmented souls. You may not realize this because you are not in touch with your inner spirit. Do you take time to ask yourself what you should do, how you should proceed? Do you listen as your mind, body and spirit process the response? Most of you use logic to arrive at a conclusion. Although logic serves a great purpose, if you use it without compassion, grace and respect, the answer can be dramatically different than what it really should be. The way people make decisions and live their life will begin to change. They will not be able to ignore their hearts; their compassion will become too loud to ignore. This will allow them to make smarter decisions.

"I know this all sounds wonderful and those who want to transform will experience this. Even those honest souls who may be ignorantly unaware will slowly progress in this direction.

"Despite this abundance of light, there will be an increase in the dark as well. I don't say this to scare you, only to help you see that you must begin to trust all your senses and intuition. There will be some who will retreat to the 'dark side' which will be inhabited by people who fear this change, who close off their senses and heart, and turn to evil to gain power. Just like the broken souls I spoke of earlier, this too can change in the presence of Love."

Barney

"Ladies always catch my attention and I can't help but want to reach out and touch them."

Barney - Java Macaque

"How do you humans move so easily with such a long body? I just can't figure it out. I keep waiting for you to fall over, but you move pretty well for being so out of proportion. Your arms are so short. I just love to watch people. They are so colorful. They wear different things on their head (hair) and things on their body that are pretty. I especially like to see what is under the colorful things, and I like things that sparkle and jangle. Ladies always catch my attention and I can't help but want to reach out and touch them. They have a way of getting my attention that I really like."

Mirabella

"I am determined and confident. I don't feel I am missing anything because I can't see. Quite the contrary really."

Mirabella – Tortoise Shell Cat (blind)

"I do not consider that I have any limitations. This is the biggest thing that I want to share with people. I am determined and confident. I don't feel I am missing anything because I can't see. Quite the contrary, really. I can sense things that most of you can't. It amazes me that you don't hear what I hear. I feel that in a way you are the ones with disabilities. The range of things I feel and sense is something that you will never experience. I feel sad for you.

When I sense things, I can see them in my mind, so for most purposes I do feel I can "see." I will always approach things in my life with a willingness and a sense of 'Yes I can'. My lack of sight will not stop me from being all cat and that is why I run outside every chance I get. I still want to experience all the pleasure that being outside has to offer. It is like a party for my senses."

Do you realize how dangerous being outside is for a blind cat, and that you must stay inside and appreciate it safely from behind a screen?

"Just try to stop me. I don't accept 'no'."

Three days after this conversation with Mirabella, she somehow slipped out of the house late one evening when we were letting the dogs in. I never realized she was missing until the morning when she did not come greet me with her morning chatter. My heart sank as I frantically searched the house for her. I quickly realized she was not stuck somewhere in the home, but must have escaped out the door. That means this vulnerable blind kitty was out all night. My husband and I searched for two days, walking the neighborhood and woods. I was slowly losing faith and fearing the worst. Friends all felt she was alive-and close, but I was too filled with fear to trust my connection and know for sure. Then I heard a voice say "Do you believe in miracles?" It was not Mirabella's voice but a voice from my guides I believe. I kept hearing it through the day. That night my husband and I concentrated on searching the woods and to my delight I saw her beautiful face emerge. She was stuck in the woods underneath all the underbrush and brambles, and every time she tried to move, she felt trapped by the overgrown earth. Her voice was just too parched to call out to me when I called to her. That night I thanked God for small miracles. You may think that after such a scare Mirabella would steer clear of the doors, quite the contrary!

Harley

"I am particularly in tune to the swirls of energy that present themselves here. Cascading swirls of brightly colored energy. It can be mesmerizing sometimes."

Harley – Bobcat

Tell me about yourself.

"I am like a 'detector' here. I can detect anything. I am always on alert. My hair, eyes, ears, and nose are constantly picking up information from my surroundings, the other animals, and the weather and energy all around. I am particularly in tune to the swirls of energy that present themselves here. Cascading swirls of brightly colored energy can be mesmerizing sometimes. They will just flow around the place and sometimes stop at certain enclosures. I think that they are either working with the animal they are near or even healing them. They have not stopped to visit with me yet, but I see them. I have seen these swirls follow people around too. They have no idea it is even happening, yet I see it all.

"I would say I am one of the 'alerters' here. My job is to sense any changes that we need to be aware of. I am constantly on duty. I can be aware if two animals on opposite ends of the sanctuary are at odds with each other. I know if there is an illness or if it is someone's birthday. I know it all because that is my job. I transfer my knowledge up to the head animals here at Tigers for Tomorrow. The head animals are Benny (leopard), Furry (lion), and Kazuma (lion). Kal-el (lion) says he is a head animal, but I have not heard this from the real heads yet.

"Everything is in order here. We know who is in charge, who are the guardians and gatekeepers, who are the alerters, the welcoming committee, the light keepers, the anchors, the counselors, comedians and ambassadors. We know our jobs and our place. This is why there is so much peace here. We are all equal in the eyes of the caretakers, that is why there is harmony. We have our own society. Not as separate groups of species, but as a whole. It works. We also have help from the spirits, and this is another area that I can discuss in detail with you as well.

"We have many animals in spirit that patrol the property. They exist in much the same way as the living do. I can see them at times. There is a lion and a wolf who head up the spirit society. They are joined by many Native Americans. Rituals are performed to heal the land here. This healing is powerful and extends out to vibrate through the core of the earth, the souls of the people and into the heart of the land. I feel this powerful vibration when it is happening. We all do. It is loud and smelly at times. Not in a bad way, but they burn sage, and there is music and chanting. There is roaring and howling, not just here, but from the spirit species as well.

"There is a powerful energy field here. It goes from deep in the earth to the sky. It is an axis or sphere of energy. If you get caught in this vortex and are of weak mind and spirit you could pass quickly. I've seen this happen. Fine one day, gone the next. It is a conscious choice. It's only accessible at certain times. We don't fear this, we respect it. Those who enter this energy sphere do it for a reason, not by accident. Wow, you don't know this? Can't you see this where you live? I'm tired of talking about this now. I have some work to do."

AnnaBelle

"Forgiveness is a beat of the heart. Without forgiveness the heart cannot beat fully and cannot love fully. Forgiveness is essential to experience all that the heart has to offer."

AnnaBelle – Tiger

"I have experienced extremes in my life. I have felt fear and pain, and as a result I show distrust and aggression outwardly. But I am intelligent enough to know when to rethink my actions, and to realize that not all things are bad, not all things hurt, and not all things will end up negatively. Once I understood this, things started to change for me. Now I am really something - perhaps one of the most gifted tigers in this place. Of course I say this not to upset the others because many will say they are more special. But I am gifted."

How are you gifted?

"I can show the most extreme aspects of a tiger's nature, yet know when to use them correctly. Sounds simple, but it is not. I know that I am privileged and that good behavior has earned me this. I love the fact that I know this and my handlers and caretakers trust me. Just like people, animals that show extremes of their personality can be classified as a bit crazy. As long as we know what is acceptable and when to act a certain way, it is not crazy.

"Forgiveness is what changed me. I chose to forgive what happened to me in the past. Forgiveness is a beat of the heart. Without forgiveness the heart cannot beat fully and cannot love fully. Forgiveness is essential to experience all that the heart has to offer. It is the essential building block of moving forward in life. To overcome hurdles in life, forgiveness must always be an option. Those who cannot feel forgiveness take years off their life, not only physically but spiritually as well."

What have you learned from your experiences with people?

"The biggest lesson is that people are not all alike. This is a mistake that many animals make - assuming all people are the same. Like animals, people react poorly out of fear and distrust. What I've learned from my handlers is that despite my poor behavior due to fear and distrust, my "person" never gave up on me. Sue kept trying and trying to get me to like and trust her. I thought she was crazy.

"And then something clicked. I realized there was no ill intent, that her main goal was for me to be happy, to feel safe, and to be less distrustful. To me, this person showed me an unwavering determination. Sue would not take 'no' for an answer, and I finally realized this and figured we could join forces and show them all that we can change. I changed because I wanted to, not because of some treat, or redundant training, but because I wanted to explore what it was this person was so insistent on getting me to know.

"I am a terrific gal."

What is your advice for people?

"I think too many people are pulled in too many directions. They are so scattered, so burned out. If they focus on something they want to accomplish and plug away at it without a set time frame, just with a determination of what they want in the end, then people would be able to do many more great things with less stress. Things would eventually fall into place, and they would be happier. You know stress is pollution. We see it, we feel it, and we know it. We animals can do nothing to help you. You have to find a way to 'mainstream', to focus your attention and let life's other debris be swept away. Stress looks like polluted air floating around a person's energy. It is not a sharp energy with a vibration; instead it is stagnant, heavy and dark. It slows down the flow of good energy, and creates sludge of sorts. Yuk.

"When I see someone who has too much of this, I bark them away, or look the other way. I don't want them to leave any of that stuff near my area. 'Take it away,' I say. If people connected more with nature, many of these stresses would go away. Nature is like a natural cure for stress. So simple, yet people continue to operate in environments that are unhealthy. They let their minds control their spirit. That's all mixed up. When I see a person who is balanced they appear to me with a clear energy field, a lovely vibration to it, and soft hues of color mixed through. The body, mind, and spirit are aligned. I know this when I see a light at the top of the head. Not many people appear this way. But there are a few. People need to aspire to this. Less stress pollution will translate into surprising benefits for all."

Ayla

"It is the young that allow Hope to show its relevance."

Ayla- Tiger

"I can see into the future. I know that youth brings hope. Your species needs hope. You will cling to whatever it is that makes you feel good, makes you feel connected, and makes you feel loved. Youth is all of those things. It is the young that allow Hope to show its relevance. When the world has crumbled around you, and all that you have built is lost, Hope is important. Don't fall prey to the call of the masses. Fall back into your heart and the rhythm of knowing you can exist fully using the earth and all her gifts. I am a beacon of hope. I will stand for this as many animals do. My heart and tenacity will link many lives together in order to bring about a change greater than yourselves. You may not realize it now. But I know my true purpose here, and you will see how my name will be known by many… Ayla."

Ayla was gifted to Tigers For Tomorrow by T.I.G.E.R.S. in Myrtle Beach, SC. Her name means healer. Sue felt it was appropriate to keep the name because at the time she was just starting to physically heal from radiation treatments.

Kal-el

"I am why people come here. They can't wait to see me. I embody what a lion should be. They can't believe their eyes when they see me. "A Lion," they say. That's right, watch me now. I can be silly too. If you're lucky, you'll see it."

Kal-el - 11 weeks old

Lady Ruby

"I feel a rumbling and uneasiness, similar to a hungry stomach below the dirt, deep in the earth."

Lady Ruby – Red Fox

"The earth feels different to me. There is a vibration under the ground that is more constant now. I feel a rumbling and uneasiness, similar to a hungry stomach below the dirt, deep in the earth. It bothers me some, but not all the animals seem as concerned as I am. Maybe because I am small and close to the earth, I sense these things more. I worry about the earth splitting from the constant vibration I feel. What started as slight has become more insistent and stronger. Do you think the earth can split from this? I sense a cracking and dryness coming as well. I can see this, flashes of it at times. I worry that we will not have water. Do you think this could happen?

"There is a sound that comes from the earth as well, like a deep moan, built-up energy cycling upward. I fear it will roar out of the earth. I have also seen flashes of heat and dryness coming. I see the earth cracking and an upheaval of energy billowing upward to the sky from below. My mouth gets dry and parched just thinking about this. Perhaps this will not happen but the vibration from below is stronger. I am not sure what will silence the monster below. Stay close to the earth, where it is most natural. There is safety in numbers and we feel safe here."

Luke

"The will is the outermost layer of the soul or spirit. It is, in many cases, what differentiates between survival and death."

Luke – Spotted Leopard

Do you have a message for humanity?

"I am very proud to be a cat of many colors. We go through many phases of realization through our physical body, changes that cause us to stop and listen and redirect our thought process or instincts. I am now in the final phase of my physical body. An older body weighs heavily on the free spirit of a cat. Our physical body and speed are things we rely on, and when illness and pain takes over, it leaves us in a very vulnerable state. It plays games with us, a constant distraction that leaves us feeling even weaker.

"In my youth, I was all about being spectacular in every way. If I thought it, I did it. My body was amazing and it gave me a sense of confidence. Now if I think it, my body is not as fast and may not be able to do it the way I used to. This leaves me in an unbalanced state of being, emotionally and instinctually. I am vulnerable. Although I was once athletic and keen, now I lay still and use my voice to warn. Oh, I can still move but I remember the power I once had. I desperately try to keep it a secret that I'm not what I once was. Some of us do this by becoming more verbal, more needy, more aggressive, or more irritable.

"I do not like the feeling of pain as it slowly creeps into my perfect body. I hate losing control of something that was once untouchable, perfect and sleek. It is a battle within that we fight. And then there comes a point when we no longer want to fight this fight. We submit or give in or resign. That is when it is time to allow our spirit to slip from a body that can no longer serve a purpose. That is when the shimmer of vibrancy behind gold eyes is lost. That is when we are called home. When you see eyes change from curious and vibrant to pleading and vacant, it is time to evaluate what it is you see. Do not keep a spirit in a body just for the sake of it. Find out if that animal is being held prisoner in a body that is ill.

"In the wild this is all taken care of for us, but here the humans have to make this decision for some of us. Not all animals want to fight the fight. Not all of us want to remain at all costs. Some prefer to exit before the weight of an ill body eats away at their soul.

"What is the will of the animal? That is what you must ask yourself. If the will is strong, and they want to fight, then yes, help them. If the will has waned, many times the body will weaken at a faster pace. When the will has left, the body has no strength left to fight, and the end is inevitable. Will is everything. I have seen animals come from situations that have left them with little to hope for, and then they experience the care and love that the people here have for them. Then you see the will and the spirit return to their eyes. And I have seen animals who were loved and cared for a long time fight a battle within their body that they no longer wish to do, and the will to live changes to the will to leave. Our will develops on a soul level and then affects all things outward. The will is the outermost layer of the soul or spirit. In many cases it is what differentiates between survival and death."

Towzer the Magnificent

"Our stripes tell a story, much like the whiskers on a lion.   We are far less subtle.   I am the king of Tiger Row.   I love to observe people."

Towzer - Tiger

"Lions may be the king of the jungle, but we Tigers are the color and pizzazz of the wild. We exhibit color, grace and strength - all of which happens in an instant. Lying outstretched in the sun is pure satisfaction for us."

Ellie

"Cats make people stop and give love. We are pretty good at insisting it. When else do people do this except with a cat?   We tell them to sit still, bend down, reach over and to stroke our gorgeous coat.   When people do this, they stop and give love.   They are allowed to give and receive love from one of the most beautiful sources in the world, a cat.   So when we run under your feet, jump on your lap, call your name, stop what you are doing, and get some love therapy."

Pockets

"I am outspoken, but I can be that way because I am so handsome."

Pockets - Green Tipped Macaw

Do you communicate with the other birds on the property, such as Sierra the Hawk and Artemis the Owl?

"I consider myself a civilized bird! They are wild. I am very valuable to people and they really enjoy my company. I help them through the day and just truly bring them joy and inspiration with my colors. The wild ones don't have the beauty that I do, so they are not for show as I am. I can be a bit picky and particular about things. I am not shy when it comes to letting people know when they are doing things the wrong way. I am outspoken, but I can be that way because I am so handsome.

"I like things to happen in sequence and when they don't, I get upset. I run a lot of things here. I am a manager.

"I am not shy about spouting my emotions. If I am unhappy with something, oh...they will know. But I am handsome and quite affectionate when needed. The ladies really love me. I am a pretty boy."

Do you have any advice as to how people can communicate better with animals and birds?

"Always start with a compliment!"

Tigger

Can you tell me what it is like being in spirit?

"What I distinctly remember about shifting out of my body is the feeling of being weightless. I felt as if I was in a hollow tunnel, and it seemed to echo. I began thinking about when I was a young cub. I was quite small and I could see my mother. Then I felt immediately filled with what I can describe as a type of exhilaration and excitement. At that moment everything sparkled and glowed. I felt like a cub as I awoke to a realm of beauty. My mother was there, she licked me. I was at home, and I felt at peace. I did not sit still for long, and I began to explore. There were limitless things to see. If I thought I would like to walk by the mountain, I was instantly in that place. My lungs were full of the breath of light, and I have never felt better. I relived everything I had ever done."

Gulliver

Llama

"The human race has been put in a position over the years to enable a change to occur both personally and globally. This can have dramatic effects if enough people follow through and speak of it. The animals cling tight to the earth's energy. It is our substance. We all play a vital role in its survival. Humans can help in this vital matter. They can reverse the damage they have done and help to heal the earth so she may grow with us. To vibrate at a level that will allow those who know, those who see, to experience true love and joy. You will not see it in your lifetime. But these coming years are important. These years will forge a path, a path for millions to follow. Where does this path lead, you ask? To a bright future? Those who want the healing to take place, truly, in their heart and soul, will help forge this path. You must live it and breathe it. We are all energy in physical bodies. As we vibrate at a higher frequency we will be able to experience what others feel, to experience their full being, just by wanting to feel it. Once we get to this level, we will banish prejudice, racism, and judgment. Instead you will look upon others with love and compassion and give them the love they need to change and respect their true self. The more people who enlist love as their weapon will help change this world. Our physical bodies anchor us to this world so that we may carry out our purpose here. If we could actually see each being's soul, there would be no hate.

"Communication with the energy in each living thing is a leap in the right direction. Listen to what we have to say, absorb our ancient knowledge and wisdom. This is the start of being able to live in a world you have only dreamed of, a world where compassion and love rule each being. As the quest for truth unfolds before your eyes, our heart's love overshadows the negative. It is a divine world, and you are welcome to it."

Cody

Cody - Black Bear

"I really do like people. I want to be very clear on this. I enjoy watching them. I like the fact that they get great joy in the simple things I do, like eating my fruit or walking around. I think it is funny that they have such great fear around us, but at the same time are amused at our simplest things.

"I have had close relationships with people. I have been hurt, not physically, but my heart has been broken before. I enjoy my life here. I enjoy getting lots of attention. There are other bears that are a bit more rowdy than me. I am pretty easy going, I would say. The others make a lot of noise and clamber for the crowd."

Cody, do you have a message for humanity, what is it that you would like people to know?

"I wish sometimes that I was small. Not so big, but small so that I could stay in the house maybe. I would like to be something different than a bear. I know that sounds odd, but we get a bad reputation sometimes. I don't want to eat people, and that is what they think sometimes. I think if I was really small, they wouldn't fear me so much. I would like to have special privileges and be able to walk around the place. But I think that I can't because I am a bear and I am a big bear. Some of the tigers and lions think that the bears are not as smart as them. They think that the feline is much smarter and quicker than the bear. I disagree with them. I think that we express our intelligence in different ways."

Do you have any messages for people?

"People are always guarded. Not my caretakers, but the people who come to see me. They are guarded. They don't like to be exposed. I watch them, and I get to know just by their body language and their thoughts the ones who are afraid to open up. They are very closed and guarded. These are the ones I will stare at sometimes. Shouldn't I be guarded toward them? I think that things are all backwards sometimes."

Finnegan

"We are a species made up of heart and pride. We work though our pain so that we can continue to please. We may not be as good as we were, but we try hard to do what we once did. We don't wish to disappoint."

Finnegan – 22 year old Thoroughbred

"As we get older and show signs of age, we don't want to feel less than worthy. I worry about the older animals I meet. We are a species made up of heart and pride, so we work through our pain so we can continue to please. We may not be as good as we were, but we try hard to do what we once did. We don't wish to disappoint. We work through the pain and suffer silently later. We hope that you will not notice our bodies slowing down. We are stoic creatures. But sometimes in the silence of our stall or paddock, we worry that one day we will not be what you want anymore. We worry that we will not meet your standards... and then what?

"I know my fate and destiny is to be with my person, Deb, forever and I take comfort in this. I still worry that someday I may not be able to do what I once did. I wonder about the others who worry that they will have no place to go. Many horses suffer in silence through physical and emotional pain to continue to please. This is what I want to bring to light, to make sure people acknowledge the older animals. They are special in their own way. And just because they may not be able to perform at the level they once did, their jobs can be changed so that their worth and wisdom is never taken for granted or over-looked."

I have been Finnegan's person since he was a 4 year old skinny and spooky horse off the race track. It was love at first sight. We had many struggles, like any relationship does, but as we both matured, we became like an old married couple. We know each other so well that we are finally comfortable with one another on all levels. Finnegan put me back in touch with a part of myself that I had somehow lost. He also helped put me on my path to animal communication along with many other smart choices I made along the way, thanks to his influence. We are bonded for life. Finnegan will be 23 soon, and although he looks terrific, he prefers to leave all that hard work to the "young ones."

Finnegan and Deb

Artemis

"I love my name. Names are important. They carry a lot of energy and projection that you may not be aware of."

Artemis – Great Horned Owl

Artemis was very polite when I connected with him and asked if he had anything he would like to share. Then he got very excited and this is what he had to share:

"I love my name. Names are important. They carry a lot of energy and projection that you may not be aware of. I do not trust people unless they approach me and tell me their name first. I love when they say my name, but I also want to hear what their name is. I read the energy and pictures behind each name that tells me a lot about who they are. Say my name, say your name, it is simple.

"I love when young humans (kids) come to see me. They interest me and I am hoping to help them to learn. That is part of my job, you know, to teach. I want to know their names though. Tell them this."

When I chatted with Artemis it was getting late and I was quite tired, so I asked him if we could finish our talk later, and he told me he was just coming alive and so he kept talking.

"It seems as if the trees fall prey to a lot of disregard and illness. They are not made like they used to be. They fall into disease more easily and are not as resistant to things. They fall prey to humans too often, getting cut down before their prime. They often do not get a chance to grow strong and this is why the new trees are so weak. I know that people don't know the trees the way I do, but if they know better maybe they will do better as well."

Indian

"Disease serves many purposes that you may not know. It challenges the very spirit to a war of wills, faith, and tolerance. It is one of our greatest lessons here on earth."

Indian – Tiger in Spirit

"Disease does not just happen. Disease is accompanied by a loss of the body's communication with the resources that have the ability to heal. Fragmented currents of communication allow the disease to grow in isolation without interruption.

"Fragmented currents are caused by many different things. They can be healed if the intention is such and if the fragments are not too far gone. We see fragmented currents as a blocking of energy, a lump of dark sludge in the body, or even a different vibration or sound.

"Any type of stress, whether environmental, emotional, or physical, can cause disease. The earlier it is corrected the better the chance of turning it around. Some diseases are aggressive, some passive. It depends on the source.

"There are times when a spirit knows that it is time to leave the earthy plane. When this decision is made on the spirit level, it consciously allows for the disease to infiltrate the body.   In so many cases, we believe the disease came first, when in fact it was the spirit's decision to leave that opened the door for earthly disease to enter the body.   I am a prime example of this. I existed to experience a wondrous place where I lived.   I saw it evolve, but then my time was up and I knew this.   Sometimes we have to leave so we can come back in a timely manner.

"Disease serves many purposes that you may not know. It challenges the inner spirit to a war of wills, faith, and tolerance.   It is one of our greatest lessons here on earth."

Mr. Lion

"It is amazing to me how naïve humans are when it comes to us. We don't live for their entertainment. We are in this preserve because of their misguided efforts to make us into something we are not, such as an attraction, a spectacle of fur and color. We are so much more."

Mr. Lion

Do people understand that animals are gifts from God? Equal in value to humans?

"Some of us are here to rescue people, to save their souls from being forgotten. That may sound dramatic to some, but animals embody the purest of emotions. They teach people how to become grounded, true, and connected. We feel the connection to the earth. Some of us are selective and choose one or two people to work with. Others touch many lives. We awaken people to the connection to all that is. We open hearts and infuse them with compassion and truth. We can see through the human layers and love unconditionally.

"I am a magnificent lion.   Lions represent dignity and order.   Each section of this preserve is represented by a lion, which is an honor."

Bubba

Bubba – Gray Wolf

"Wolves are the keepers of the land. We travel in groups and prefer to be with family. We are also aware of some changes to come. The 'Great Blackness' as we call it, will be upon us in this lifetime. It will be a time of darkness, more than we are used to. People will need to learn to be one with the land and animals in order to survive. The light will shine again, but those who are forced to live without their conveniences will miss the opportunity at this time to evolve."

Grumpy

Grumpy – Kinkajou

What a nice home you have here. Do you ever wish that Honey (the other Kinkajou) could be in with you full time?

"I love having my own space. This gives me the opportunity to get 'up close and loving' with my person. I don't want to share my space full time with Honey (female Kinkajou). She is much too bossy and would try to tell me what to do. I would have to get angry at her. I don't mind spending some time with her for short periods, but usually my person can tell when enough is enough and she removes Honey. I am quite relieved that she understands this and does not leave her with me longer than I want. Honey tries to change things around and takes over my nest (bed)."

You like your man cave!

"I like having a place where my person can come and go, without having to compete with another for attention. Honey can be very temperamental, and I do not wish to present myself that way. I've worked very hard to allow people into my heart. I am proud of this and want to keep going in the right direction."

Tsunami

"No matter what you encounter in this life, you will always have your spirit.
When you forget that, you will be finished."

Tsunami – Tiger

"Tigers embody the spirit of the wild. We should not be declawed, caged, or mounted as trophies for your enjoyment. I am here for all people to know that I am wild and free in my mind. You can never take that away from me. People can learn from this."

"Your spirit is the embodiment of your creation, so fan that flame and let it shine bright. If you do, you will attract the light to you. I do not crouch in fear anymore. I am here to enlighten and don't take my job lightly. It is an honor to represent my species. I am the first on 'tiger row' and my home is in my heart. I am wild and free.

"Benny the Leopard lives next to me. When visitors come my way, he tells me what their issues may be. I work to see deep inside people. Many have experienced pain and abuse. I find this interesting. For such a smart species, many humans lack a foundation of inner strength. Their souls are weighed down by many things. Benny has helped me see this."

Pepper

"I am going to be the show stopper soon, very soon. I love to entertain and want an audience. I am cute, smart, and everyone knows it. Yonah, the Grizzly Bear, teaches me a lot. I want to be just like him."

Pepper – Black Bear

Magic

Magic - Tiger

"The majesty of my being is the ability to forget my past. This way I see myself once again through the heart of a human. It is hard to see your reflection when the heart cannot reflect. A heart that is dark cannot reflect because there is no light. I have known both kinds of hearts. I am happy now to see my reflection in a way I never thought possible. That was perhaps my greatest accomplishment - never losing hope in what humans call love."

Spike

I had the pleasure of meeting Spike at Octagon Wildlife Sanctuary in Punta Gorda, Florida. He was a chatty fellow with a fun personality. He would constantly show me mental pictures of the things he wanted and he loved holding court with his onlookers.

Spike – Baboon

"I could sit and talk all day. I love hanging out with humans. They really like my company as well. I would like a big swing in the middle of my enclosure so that I can swing with my feet in the air. It should be soft not hard. I love to watch TV and like certain voices more than others. I would love more things to make music with.

"I really do run things here and know just what is happening. I like things to be on a timely schedule and don't like it when I have to wait for food. I think Spike should come first."

Is there anything you need or want?

"I am male, but I am nurturing. I really want a baby to hold and take care of, maybe a rabbit baby. I also miss being cradled and hugged. I love to be hugged and rocked. My person is very busy, and I love to spend time with her. She is my light each day. Nothing would make sense without her love and dedication to me and my lifestyle. I admit I am demanding and want her to come when I call. She listens well. I really love to be loved. This makes me whole.

"I would also like more green foods to peel, *(he shows me something that looks like an artichoke)*. I also love pizza, but I can't get it that often. It is a special treat between me and my person. I love to be read to and cherish the times people come and sit with me. Sometimes they hum to me as well. I am just a big baby. I love people of the female persuasion. They are all pretty to me and have nice voices."

After this conversation, Spike's person bought him some artichokes which he thoroughly enjoyed. She admitted that every Thursday night is pizza night, and sometimes she shares her piece with him. She also confirmed that there is a woman who comes weekly and sits outside of Spike's enclosure and reads.

Katie

"I don't have a lot of respect for a lot of people.   They make bad choices and they probably taste bad too!"

Katie – Tiger

Willow

Willow - Cougar

"We are aware of the earth's changes. We have seen the warning signs and we must alert the others. Be prepared for unstable times."
(Willow telepathically showed me the earth rumbling and cracking twice in a short period of time.)

"The middle of the Americas will be challenged *(she shows me all this through mental images)*. It will be more disruptive than you can imagine. There will be violent storms and mud slides. Tornadoes will increase in energy, and strong storms will increase in number.

"Native American people with heavy spirits will congregate in certain areas of sacred land, in an attempt to bless the land. They heal the sores that others have created on this great earth. Their tears will rain down on us."

Lilly

Most times when I communicate with an animal, it is a barrage of pictures and scenes that they choose to show me along with words, thoughts and feelings. Sometimes the words come so fast that it is hard to keep up with them. In a few cases, the animal's voice is so distinct that it becomes a part of their personality. I had a horse who drawled out every word with a John Wayne type sound, and a Rottweiler with a deep voice like Barry White. Lilly is one of those animals who speaks with a very distinct tone. Her voice was velvety smooth with a hint of flirtiness.

Lilly – Black Leopard

"I love the seasons of the moon. Most people wait for sunrise to start living the day but I truly love the moon. The sun is the same each day but the moon... well, that changes all the time. The moon has a different energy each night. The night is not for everyone, though. I think a lot of people and some animals really miss the electric feeling that comes upon the middle of the night. It is like living on the edge. Of course I am completely safe behind my walls, but I let my mind wander... I imagine there are no walls and I am waiting to pounce on something, or perhaps I need to run from something. It is quite fun."

"I love the mornings as well. That is a good time for people to get the best from me. I am talkative and playful, but in the afternoon I prefer to nap away from the heat of the sun. So if you really want to experience my true personality, you need to get up early or come very late. I think another thing people need to know is that we communicate fluently with our tails. We don't just wave them around for the fun of it, the tail moves in response to our thoughts. So you can tell a lot just by how our tails move. Straight up and waving indicates curiosity, but tapping on the ground means look out."

Boris

"When people walk by me, they should stand back, and "ooooo" and "ahhhh" at how great I am, then move on."

Boris - Lion

"I am Boris. You may not want to repeat what I tell you as it could be offensive, but I love to mess with the visitors. Yes I do! It is my entertainment. I like to make fun of their hats, the colors on their bodies, what they carry, what they expect me to do, and how they stumble with their awkward bodies. I make all the others laugh. I warn them as they come strolling our way and act like a big bad lion sometimes. I will ignore them, or yell at them, it depends on my mood. I love to make Cowboy, my tiger friend next door, laugh. He can't see well, so I fill him in on the details. People are quite dumb - is that the right word? They just walk around, not really understanding much, looking at us as if we are on display and saying things they think we don't understand. I just want to yell, "Hey, I can hear you!"

"I told you this may be offensive, but I am Boris, the Great. When people walk by me, they should stand back, and "ooooo" and "ahhhhh" at how great I am, then move on. Cowboy, the tiger next door, likes people. I only like the elite group of caretakers who love and serve me. But I will admit that if people didn't come to see us, I think I would be very bored. I can't make fun of Cowboy too much, he takes it to heart.

"We are treated like kings here, as we should be. I will tell you that the other animals here, if they dare, do make fun of me at times. I am a napper, and when I doze, they sometimes think I am dead. It is funny to hear them chattering away, "who's gonna tell Sue and Wilbur he's dead?" I just love to nap.

"And I like to eat, but my tooth is bothering me lately. So you see, my child, Lions command respect, yet we also can reflect back to people things which they can't understand and make them look silly. That is what I enjoy."

Ravi

Ravi – Golden Tabby

Do you realize that your species is becoming extinct?

"I realize that I am one of a few. I can tell this by what people say and what many of the animals know, especially the Tigers. I live among a lot of them, but I am young. I'm still the baby to some. One day the scope of all of this may make sense but right now they make sure that I have fun and experience all the ranges of life and play. They don't ever want me to feel like an object in a cage on display. No, I am Ravi."

Sheila

Female Chimpanzee

"I feel emotions the same as people do, maybe even more so, because at times I suffer silently, alone with my feelings in a world too big for me to understand. My heart still aches. I think the pain will never go away. I lost my friend and the sorrow I feel is real. I miss her touch and her all encompassing love. I miss when she would kiss my head and hold my hand. We were quite a pair. I miss that. But she told me to take care of things here and that is what I am doing. I like to know what is going on at all times and don't like surprises! I watch all that comes and goes, and keep an eye on the youngsters. She would be proud of this.

"I don't always see myself as others do. No, I feel much prettier than that. I am different than others in my species, and feel more human-like at times. I know they understand me, and I understand them. I miss my blanket; I want my people to know. I had a special blanket, and I miss it. When things are changed or moved, I don't like it."

Tawny

Tawny - Tiger

"Sometimes we are meant to be alone. People can be over-stimulating to us, or maybe just to me. When I make a decision, I stick to it. Some can be convinced otherwise, not me.

"I am very private and do not wish to discuss things that have pained me. I know I am safe now, but still prefer to be away from the public eye.

"I see my life in two different parts, 'not knowing' and 'knowing'. I am in the 'knowing' stage now. Most of the time, I keep to myself. I do admit to loving the night time when all is quiet. I can sometimes hear people off in the distance, people I know. When it is dark out, the outside energy has subsided, things shift to quiet, and I sit and enjoy that feeling. I feel safe in the night."

<u>Pongo</u>

Pongo – Male Orangutan

"I am a mighty guy. I enjoy my spot at this place because I like to talk to my friend across the way *(he shows me another smaller monkey)*. He lets me know when a group of people are coming around the corner. Sometimes I get up and get their attention, and sometimes I lie still so that they will draw their attention to my smaller friends. I am not just any orangutan, I AM PONGO. Everyone knows my name because I am very special here. I have to be reminded of my strength, though. I truly do not always realize how strong I am and have a hard time controlling myself when I get upset. I do not like things changed.

"I love my buddy across the way, we have a lot of fun. I look out for him and I am so glad he is here."

Champp

"Love conquers the darkest soul, the deepest pain, and the most broken spirit.
Open your heart so that the wings of love can fly."

Champ – Pitbull mix in spirit

Champ was left for dead at a home we were preparing to purchase. He was kept in a small caged area outside and pans of rotten food lay strewn about the area. He drank out of a green slime covered children's pool and was skin and bones. We told the owners of the home we would buy it on the condition that the dog would come with it. We found out from neighbors that Champ escaped regularly to romance the female dogs and was known to many as "the Mayor." Champ was one of those beings that exemplify a dog's unconditional love and honor. He never let his ill fated past affect his present and he always started each day with a big smile and enthusiastic joy. We feel so lucky to have had him in our lives for the time that we did. He continues to be one of the greatest teachers I know. He was a saint in a dog's body.

Yonah

"I am a gentle being with a curious heart. The challenge is being in such a massive body that people mistake as a constant threat."

Yonah – Male Grizzly Bear

<u>Sam</u>

"I am not really good at following the rules because I forget them."

Sam - Mixed Breed

Sam is one of the most persistent beings I have ever met. He has insisted since we started talking about this book that he would be a part of it. He wanted to travel with us to visit all the animals and watch over Sue. Sam is the youngest dog at the preserve. He knows when he has done something wrong, which is often, and admits that he just can't help it. Because of Sam's persistence, I decided to connect with him to see what it was that he had to share with people for the book. This is what he wanted to say:

Deb, Sam and Sue

"I run, I run, I run, sometimes I run in circles to get away from my past. I think that the faster I run, I can leave my past behind. It still catches up with me no matter how dizzy I get in trying to lose it."

What is it you are trying to run from?

"I fear being lost and being left behind. I want to be with my person Sue always. I worry that I will be taken away. The pain of this separation would rip me in two. I'm scared that I will not be able to find her and that I will be alone."

"My past stalks me and whispers in my ear to be afraid, and that makes me nervous and unsettled. It is a thorn in my side, jabbing me and keeping me ever vigilant."

The past is just that, the past. You need to acknowledge that it happened and live forward now. You need to have more confidence in your purpose here and what you have now. Once you do that, the past will become less disturbing to you and eventually will fall into a distant memory.

"I need everyone to take me seriously. I am on a mission to protect and serve my person Sue. They all just need to get out of my way; I need to run things here. I am the boss."

Once you honor the rules everyone follows for the good of all, you will be taken more seriously and afforded more freedom to do your job.

"I am not really good at following the rules because I forget them. But I will try. I admit I like to cut to the chase. I tell the other dogs the rules are for them and that I am special. It is hard when I get in trouble. They laugh at me, then I have to go back out there and prove myself time and time again to them. A quick bite often does the trick. I am faster than most of them."

Sam, remember to do the right thing, even when no one is looking!

Aurora and Sam

Sierra

"See before you know…   Know before you do."

Sierra – Red Tailed Hawk

"Birds are the greatest diagnostic tool this planet has. Through our actions, migrations and habitat, you can tell a lot about certain areas of this planet. Unlike many of the animals here, I am heartbroken that I can no longer soar free. Birds are fragile beings, even the birds of prey. I want to fly."

What would a hawk want the people to know?

"I don't dislike being here. In fact I feel I am relating very well with my purpose of educating young humans. However, I still want to soar the skies, to ride the currents of the wind and to land smoothly on a tree or branch of my choosing. The winds tantalize me, and some days I grow weary.

"In closing, what I would like people to know is that they need to talk to nature more and understand the changes that I see and hear. If you talked to nature you would know that the trees are sick. I see and hear this a lot. They are sickly because there is not enough oxygen. You will begin to see these changes in increased fungus and insect infestation. We hawks work closely with the trees. Where there used to be abundance there no longer is. This holds true for many things and trickles down into your lives as well. It does not have to be this way. People must make conscious choices right down to the most simple everyday things. This is where it has to start."

After this conversation with Sierra, her caretakers learned that the trees surrounding her and Artemis's enclosure were diseased and sick and had to be removed.

Mojo

Mojo – Black Leopard

Mojo speaks in a very deep slow voice. I had asked him a few questions when I met him and after pondering them for a while, this was what he had to share.

Can animals sense climate changes and weather patterns to come?

"I am uneasy talking about this but I do sense danger coming."

(He telepathically shows me a picture of the ocean along the shoreline. As the waves lapped against the shore there were black pieces of ash or something similar being washed onto the sand.)

"There is a series of events leading up to this."

(He then shows me how the winds will pick up for weeks at a time along with some prevalent storms.)

"The sky will light up and after a time things will settle down. The earth is unsteady."

How do you know these things?

"The birds, they talk about these changes. I just listen quietly."

Will the earth be ok?

"Yes. There will be some cleanup. It will be a combined effort of human compassion to begin to clean up and rebuild. This is not a global event, but one that will touch in a global manner."

<u>Rudy</u>

"I am made of pure pride and feathers the color of royalty."

Rudy – Rooster in spirit

"Think of me as the bell tower on a church. I was the General in charge of the barn area. I was very important and I think people looked at me with a knowledge that I was special. No ordinary rooster, but a very special and handsome being. I took great pride in my job and knew how to instill order when things got chaotic out here. I may be little but the power I have goes beyond size. I am majestic as some would say. I had some problems with my wing, but it never stopped me from doing my job. Roosters are very focused. We know what our job is and how to do it. People just need to step out of the way and let us get on with it. We will always find a way, no matter what.

"I too have been through many challenges and growing pains here. I have seen many leave this place. At first it was a bit frightening seeing tigers wandering among us, then I realized they were in spirit and they were just curious what it was like to be us, farm animals. Many wander around like this after they pass, they just don't want to leave. They know that they are a part of something special. I was the one that saw them, I don't think the others did or they would have jumped the fence. I see all and know all. I still do. I sit on top of the barn and still watch over the property. I manage the rise and fall of the sun with the symphony of my voice. I holler loudly on cloudy days so the sun will become strong.

"I have witnessed storms that shook our world, and joy that did the same. When I think back on it all, it wears me out. But while I was experiencing it I just became stronger. I am a rooster - one of the mightiest beings on earth. I am made of pure pride and feathers the color of royalty."

Zena

"Even the shattered pieces of our lives can be restored.
That remedy is love."

Herk and Zena - Tigers

"I have confidence in my life now. That was not always the case. I come from broken pieces. But what I have found throughout my life is that there is one thing that can mend any broken piece. Even the shattered pieces of our lives can be restored. That remedy is love. But it is not the word 'love' that conquers all. It is so much more. It is a feeling unlike any other. And some of you may experience pieces of love, but to experience love fully is truly something else. If you stop and think about the things you love, without reservation, without conditions, with total abandonment of outcome, what would you come up with?

"For me, I am lucky. I think people find it surprising when animals love one another. They expect us to love people, but when we love one another, they think it is special. I am not sure why that is. Animals, unlike most two legged hairless creatures, understand love. They don't expect things as a result of it, they just understand it. They give it and receive it. It is when the hairless two-leggeds think they know better that things can get sticky, dirty and distorted. I know they don't know any better. What I have found in my life is that I attract good people now. Because of the love I feel and receive, I attract them into my life. I am loved by everyone here. I am respected as well. My caretakers understand all my qualities and quirks. They don't expect anything from me except to understand that all they do is in our best interest. I know this. I teach this to the newcomers here. They must understand love. Once they do, they will blossom in this place. Love should be a feeling first, a seed that grows silently inside, until it becomes strong enough to be seen and heard.

"I can tell which animals have not experienced love in their past. They are angry or fearful. They resent things. Once they allow the tiniest bit of love to be felt in their soul, then they can lift the burden of pain, doubt, fear, and anger that they carry. As I said before, these things fester inside like a disease. This disease attracts more of the same. The body and mind become diseased and the spirit is left in a prison of sorts, slowly dying inside. I don't mean to be so grim; however, I want everyone to know that the cure to it all is love. Love from the inside out. Love should extend beyond the concepts of the mind. Love should know no limit and always feel worthy of it all.

"I have seen people come and go here. I believe that the animals here are seeds. We are seeds for tomorrow. We plant seeds in people's minds, consciousness, and hearts. We plant seeds in the energy of this place as well. Helping each of us to rise above many hurdles we have endured. We are a group of beings, some may say throwaways. I have heard this term before. And some of the animals still refer to us as such. This does not bother me because it is past tense. Now we are a strong group, fighting for something much bigger than ourselves or our species. A shift in awareness is needed to understand that all of this is much bigger than ourselves. We are all connected. What you do to me, you do to you. People need to live with their hearts wide open. They need to hear with their conscience and see with their heart. Then, the change will come. I am waiting; we are all waiting… for the signs from above that we are heading in the right direction."

Miss Ollie

"Only in knowing weakness first can you truly appreciate the full scope of strength and grace. What we learn here (earth) will only enhance what you can do over there (spirit)."

Miss Ollie – Llama in spirit

Miss Ollie, do you have anything you would like to share about your life or what it is like being in spirit form?

"I thought you would like to know that when we are in spirit we have jobs, but they may not be jobs that you would expect. Some are quite different than what was suited for us when in body. For instance, I did not really want much to do with the very young animals when I was here. I enjoyed being with my companion too much. Yet in spirit that is what I do. I prepare young souls for reentry into physical form."

"Well, these young ones need looking after, and that is what I do. I gather them up and keep them in line.

"I help the young souls learn to do their job in spirit so they can face the challenges of returning to the physical plane.

"We are not born into perfection. Perfection is obtained piece by piece by handling the errors and challenges a soul may face. It is through these challenges that we may live and learn so that the knowledge and experience can be used to better ourselves on a soul level. Only in knowing weakness first can you truly appreciate the full scope of strength and grace. What we learn here in the spirit world helps us do our job when we return to the physical world."

Miss Ollie telepathically shows me through pictures that when a soul decides to reincarnate, they experience a quick reversal in age, from adult to baby, and then they enter into a body. It seems that during this time of age reversal they energetically take on the physical parameters of the body or species they are incarnating into.

Lt. Ranger Fuzzy Bear

Lt. Ranger - Black Bear in Spirit

"Some of us are not meant for captivity. We are not wired that way. I think it is quite apparent those who are and those who aren't. I am one such soul. And I knew this from the day I was born. I was meant to be climbing trees, foraging for food and handling the harsh weather as best I could."

"I know the people who found me were just trying to help me, but I desperately wanted to go back to where I came from. I was determined to make it. I missed my mother, and I wanted to be with her. I know now that she was hurt and injured. And I have recently found her in spirit and I am happy to be with her.

"When I was in body, every ounce of my being wanted to be back in the wild. This overcame my will to survive. I was not very cooperative; I was stubborn, I guess. This is what I would like for people to know; that many of my species and other species do well working with humans and living in captivity, but some of us cannot handle this, due to a broken heart or a broken will. And as a result of this, I became ill. I know my rescuers had my best interests in *their* hearts, but *my* heart could not take it."

Lt. Ranger Fuzzy Bear was a very brave little bear. It was apparent he was a wild bear and missed the wild and this broke our heart. He was moved into a small enclosure next to Cody Bear and Cody really cared for "the Fuzz." He would sit for hours across from him watching him play. When Lt. Ranger Fuzzy Bear passed, Cody grieved for his little friend for days.

Cheetah

"I leave behind a legacy that goes beyond what I have done while being in one of the most magnificent bodies I know of."

Cheetah – Chipanzee in Spirit

"The purpose of my life exists on many levels. I feel that I was one of the first to help people see the type of relationship my species can have with humans. I became known for my ability to interact with humans in a way that went beyond good training and commands to knowing what was needed, doing it, and actually enjoying the pleasure and praise I got. I was very big inside and had a very big heart. Most people saw this part of me. I was very gentle and those who knew me towards the end of my life became my family. In looking back, I can see now that I grew up too fast and was not able to enjoy being young and carefree. I missed my mother and just enjoying love for the sake of love.

"The end years of my life strangely became the best. That was when I was looked after with complete love. It was no longer about what I could do. I was allowed to just be. This was very new to me. I thought my value to humans was all about what I could do. But I found out during the last segment of my lifetime that humans are not all alike. My last home was where I found out that some humans love us, just to love us. I felt dignified once again for who I was and not what I could do. My love for these people made my heart explode. This was perhaps the greatest lesson I can recall. I leave behind a legacy that goes beyond what I have done while being in one of the most magnificent bodies I know of."

Do you have a message for the people who took care of you during the last chapter of your life?
"I am with my animal and human family here in spirit. We look after all that we have left behind. We hear your prayers and we do our best to help you through the hurdles you encounter. Remember my gentle touch on your cheek and know that I am always here. I leave you gifts on your birthday and mine. This is something fun that I love to do.

"The visions you see for my old home are great and much needed. We are moving things along on this end to make your visions a reality. Your spirit and momentum are magnified twenty times when you call on us to help. Reach out your hand and feel my hand in yours. I am with you."
"Love, Cheetah."

Cheetah lived out the last chapter of his famed life surrounded by love and support at the Suncoast Primate Sanctuary in Palm Harbor, Florida.

Isis

Isis – Gray Wolf

"Fear not, because what is coming was meant to happen. You have nothing to fear if you have moved to a place of forgiveness and love in your whole being. Those who flourish during times of fear will perish if not careful. The earth will cleanse itself, it has been overdue. The animals know this."

What changes are you talking about?

"More wind, less rain. The temperatures will be unsteady and the seasons as you know them will change. Storms with daggers of ice will create concern. Certain trees will begin to die and acid below the earth will deteriorate the soil. This will be your first clue. Birds will no longer migrate as usual, and this will disrupt many things. The bees will be confused by the changes in the plants. It will disrupt their delicate systems. The earth will self-adjust and when it does, we must start over with better intentions. When all species work together towards a common goal - the good of all - then change can be felt and seen instantly. Too many of you do not believe in this. Just because you can't see it, that doesn't mean it isn't real. We can change anything if we all act together towards a higher vibration of integrated love and harmony. From the earth to the oceans to the skies, all must be cleansed and rebuilt through the highest power of Love. God exists in each of us as Love. Yet so many don't ever tap into this amazing potential when all we need to do is ask. Find something to howl for, and then use Love to accomplish it to the highest extent possible. Love in its purest form is the source of miracles. It is where all else stems from. Fear is where the dark festers. Know this, for it is the rule of the future."

Brother

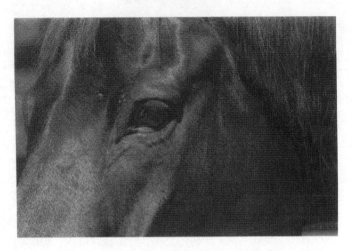

Thoroughbred Horse in Spirit

I connected with this beautiful being in spirit and was curious as to the way his energy came through. It was full of a golden light. I asked him why he has this golden light around him.

"When we pass into spirit the vibration of the soul emits a light. The stronger the vibration, the more spiritually aware and full of love the soul is. Also, different lights mean different things. For instance, Supreme Masters or Saints have an almost pure white light around them, with a crispness and tone like no other. There are many ranges of light. Golden light usually signifies a soul that made a difference on the earth plane either knowingly or unknowingly. It does not mean that one was better than the other. It is more an indicator of what was achieved. We respect this very much. It keeps us eager to evolve."

What would you like people to know about Horses?

"I would like to talk about life lessons. What it feels like to be a horse, to be misunderstood time and time again. Sometimes a horse can feel so alone that it seems it is us against the world. Sometimes you think that everyone you meet is the bad guy. In this state of mind, you can retreat and disconnect completely or explode from the inside out because it is the only way to get attention and to get the anger and frustration out. I chose the latter. First because I had a very athletic body and second because retreating is not in my nature. I stand for integrity and perseverance. My spirit and stamina are strong and I do not put up with unjust behavior lightly.

"Looking back now, I do see that when I was young people did not mean to treat me the way they did. I see now that they just didn't know better. That is sad. When you are passed around and corrected time and time again and labeled as difficult it hurts. It was really hard to do what they wanted in a body riddled with pain. But with every challenge there always is a solution if you open your eyes wide enough to see it. As I said earlier I do not retreat, and if I had I would have missed a golden opportunity to meet my person; the one who saved me.

"Although she may say that I saved her, actually she saved me, and it was meant to happen. When kindred souls find each other, no matter how broken they may be at the time, there is a chance for miracles. My miracle was a pain-free body and a relationship that far exceeded your human concept of love and commitment. I was finally understood and respected and the person who saved me gained unconditional love and her life's calling. I often wonder what would have happened had we not met. I shudder to think of the outcome for us both.

"So I am here to share the fact that horses have the unique ability to help people connect with the very thing they need at the time. We are not difficult, but we're easily misunderstood. Please do not label us "difficult" because for some that is a death sentence. But try to see things from our point of view. Try to understand that maybe it is you who has much to learn. A reflection does not lie. So if a horse comes to you, stop and take a look at yourself. What is it that you need to learn?"

Brother's person, Anne, has expressed to me that this horse was the reason she found her purpose and became a Doctor of Chiropractic. Brother was misunderstood in his younger years and labeled "wild" and "dangerous" before she bought him. Despite his reputation, she fell in love with the heart of this horse. She saw his pride and nobility and a fierce desire to be understood. Anne quickly realized that his behavior was due mostly to the significant amount of pain his body was in. She worked hard at getting his body healthy and pain free, and found the most relief for him through chiropractic. At the time she had to trailer him hours to a place where he could be adjusted and relieved of his pain. He led her to her path and now she has a very successful practice enabling humans, horses and dogs to heal in a gentle natural way. I have seen her help many animals when traditional medicine left them no hope.

Kazuma

Kazuma is an inspiration to all who meet him. He exemplifies forgiveness in the purest form. Kazuma was rescued from a traveling circus where he spent a decade of his life in a tiny cage on the back of a pickup truck. Kazuma is living out the remainder of his life with dignity and respect at the Tigers for Tomorrow Animal Preserve in Atalla, Alabama. I got to meet Kazuma in person and my eyes filled with tears the way he perked up and filled with love when Wilbur and Sue, the angels who rescued him, called his name. The love is so strong it is palpable. He is magnificent and proud and full of love thanks to his new life.

Kazuma - Lion

"My greatest fear was dying a worthless life. Now I am freed from that fear. I have a purpose and dignity. I have seen the worst and the best of being in captivity. One can take your spirit away and the other can lift it up. I am thankful for both so that I can truly savor my life now. I am worthy and I know this now."

What message do you have for people so that they can evolve?

"People want to be entertained. They have trouble just sitting back and taking in the energy of a situation. In their quest for constant entertainment, they miss the magic of just being, of just listening and experiencing a moment in time. When they rely on outside things for fun, for something spectacular to entertain them, they usually end up disappointed. They go to extreme measures to achieve this level of excitement. Herein lies the basis of their destruction, the foundation is broken. The quality of 'being' is lost. They no longer can hear... from within. They are hollow vessels, stimulated only by the outside world.

"Imagine just being able to hear the thoughts of a lion, to have a conversation with an animal that could take your life in the blink of an eye, but that chooses to sit and watch as you make a fool of yourself, taunting me inside a cage so that you can be entertained. Certainly, you are in need of training, because it is you who have lost the essentials of life. Yes, I live behind four walls, but I still cherish each moment and can be at one with the earth and with you, just by imagining such a thing. Can you even comprehend the scope of this?

"Ah, humans can be so lost. I study them because they are the cause of the rise and fall of all that is….. I am not sure why, but I think they have the biggest lesson to learn here. Humans have a great capacity to love, animals have a great capacity to forgive. Humans can join together for something they love and miracles happen. I am an example of this. All too often humans think that to love too much shows weakness when in reality it shows great strength. I choose to live in the here and now, this is why I can forgive. My present situation supersedes my past. And so it is. Thank you for listening! It is about time."

Whales

Many of the whales with whom I have had the pleasure of communicating with were located in Stellwagen Bank, a National Marine Sanctuary off the coast of Cape Cod, Massachusetts. It is home to hundreds of sea creatures including the magnificent Humpback Whale and the critically endangered North Atlantic Right Whale. This magnificent sanctuary is deteriorating a little bit every year and it is up to us to try to help protect and preserve it. Please go to www.stellwagenalive.org or www.coastalstudies.org for more information on getting involved.

Humpback Whales - Cape Cod, MA

"We journey far to keep our species alive and must travel greater distances for food. This causes us to go longer without food and travel hundreds of miles to raise our young. These are well thought-out decisions for the continuation of our kind. The ocean is not safe anymore. We have obstacles that alter our existence and survival in many ways. Adjustments have been made in our living and eating habits but not without consequence. For every adjustment made, valuable members are lost. We still delight in our journey and have made our purpose known and the significance of it felt. We love our ocean and the beings that inhabit it.

"We know when humans interact with us because we feel their love and pain. They are our hope for survival, but they have made our oceans unsafe and unclean. In the midst of this horrific disregard for life, some have let their hearts light the way to a brighter future. More humans are coming forward and making a difference. We have hummed a vibration for healing, trying to repair the ocean and the human spirit. Our survival is in many ways in your hands and your hearts. Your help is appreciated.

"Whales are wise beyond your comprehension, with layers of wisdom and information hundreds of years deep embedded in our cells. We coordinate healing circles and songs, we mourn death and extend our compassion among ourselves and also out to the humans. We experience high levels of emotion and absorb sound energy through our bodies in a way that decodes and understands every intricate detail. It is a full knowing."

"The dolphins are our brothers, our comrades in the healing of the human heart and the world. We swim together to bring about this subtle healing and opening of hearts. We touch your souls in a way you may not even realize, but you will feel the connection once it has been made. We open your heart through our struggle for survival despite fishing nets, oil spills, and pollutants. Our graceful presence and kindred spirit is what we project. In doing so, we open you up to compassion and when compassion is felt, the heart is open. When the heart is open, miracles happen.

"Whales have existed for centuries and hope to remain for centuries more. Being dangerously close to extinction, we must get your attention to help save our home. And when I say our home, I include every living thing. This connection, this oneness, is our hope for survival. The vibration level needs to be higher to save this planet. The key to this is Love.

"Soon people will begin to experience a dual consciousness. Many already have, and find this world too painful to stay in. This is why many are leaving. As we awaken to this higher level of existence we will become aware of the unity of souls. The earth is really just a reflection of the energy within ourselves, our ocean, and our world. A major upheaval is inevitable given the vulnerable condition we have put her in."

What is a dual consciousness?

"It is living in a physical world but understanding things through the eyes and heart of all; and when we awaken to this, our vibration moves up as well. As I stated before, many do this for short periods of time. The stress that this world holds makes it painful to experience this for too long. The change you will see is that many beings will stay in this dual consciousness for longer periods of time. By doing this, we are accelerating the healing of all, but we also burn out quicker because the physical body cannot withstand this for too long. The whales have taken on this burden for far too long. We have the knowledge of the universe in each cell and enter 'still point' for a longer time than any other mammal. As a result of this we have access to all that is.

"Whales are finding that being in the ocean at times is unbearable. The sonar waves at deep levels create a pressure within that can make us feel sick. We search for calmer waters to live in and spend more time at the shallow levels to escape this constant pain. Many whales find themselves beached as a result, and exhausted from the stress of this.

"We are developing unhealthy cells in our bodies due to radiation created by humans. Because we are so large and absorb so much in the fat cells of our bodies, we are more sensitive to this than humans. Humans tend to flush their bodies more easily of these toxins, but our cells allow them to remain. Then our tissues become toxic and malignant.

"Water temperatures are warmer than usual and different strains of algae are becoming more abundant. This may seem like a good thing, but it is destroying the eco balance of the ocean. For many fish, these strains can act like a virus. It is biological pollution.

"There will be many upheavals involving the earth and a major shift in consciousness for many. A 'divide', if you will. The turmoil leading to it will be reflective of the shift of energy. A 'new time,' some say another chance for humans to think of something besides themselves. Humans are stewards of the earth to protect and preserve her. What if your precious conveniences were no more? Would humans choose to give up their conveniences for the sake of saving a species, maybe a few species, or the earth as a whole? This is what we are moving towards.

"Yes... time is speeding up, oceans are heating up, the skies are unstable, and the earth is angry. The human consciousness needs a retuning. The frequency must change. This is a chant for all, not for one. There will be an exploding of a spiritual consciousness of many, as if you are finally all on the same page. Not fighting, but working together for the right cause.

"As the ocean mammals become ill, and beach ourselves, it is important for humans to probe deeper into our cause of death. In our sick cells will be the keys to help humans to heal from their diseases as well. But these can only be found when we are ill, so please do not destroy us for your research, but wait until we give our bodies to you. Then, and only then, will the information be available to you."

Bear

Bear

© R. Malin '05

Gray Wolf in spirit

Bear is a wolf I got to know at Tigers for Tomorrow sanctuary when it was located in Fort Pierce, Florida, before moving to Attalla, Alabama. Bear was very protective of Sue, and full of advice and love for her. He is an old soul, and his passing (October, 2007) was difficult for both Sue and Lakota, his mate. I was able to connect with him in spirit after his passing and this is what he had to share with me for Sue.

"There is a major shift happening here and everywhere. My spirit zipped out of my body as it was supposed to. I first fought it, but then finally gave in and when I did, I became pain free.

"I was called from the other side to return there. Lakota, my mate, may soon follow but I asked her to stay for now. There will be a new energy arising with your 'farm.' Species with very difficult problems will come. Some will have lost all faith in humans. That is what you will restore for them. The light of good in humans has been lost in the eyes of many animals. It is essential for humans to 'feel' again, so that we can all be connected again. Many animals will come who have lost faith in universal love and have been held prisoner to the ills of people. You may be the last hope that their spirit and purpose can once again be complete. You will enable them to feel love, compassion, and respect from a human. When they end up at the sanctuary, it is the start of their spiritual healing process. It brings spiritual freedom to them. Your purpose is much larger than this place.

"Bodies aside, the animals who come are here to be healed on a spiritual level. That is why you will find more of them coming. Prepare yourselves for this. Help will come to you because your work is sacred. Hawk circles the mountain and oversees all. You are both connected to American Indian wisdom and you will need to use this more and more. Call upon Hawk for direction and answers."

"When the animals in your care fall ill, do not give in to sadness. With a full heart embrace their transition, because you have healed them on a soul level. They have once again felt Love and now they are free to cross over, free to be with their ancestors, and free from any past pain. It is what their heart wanted, and they crossed over full of love.

"I have chosen to go to the spirit world at this time. It was not planned. It was a great awakening for me. I needed to make room for others who are coming. I have chosen to leave my weak body despite my fight to stay. I know that I was called to leave. I am stoic in my heart, but I love you with my whole soul.

"I am to oversee the mountain and you. I am the gatekeeper, a fearless defender of all that should be good. I have chosen to leave my body behind in order to do my job at the highest level possible at this time. You are sacred to me. I am with you, in a strong but reserved way. I will howl at night so your ears can know that I am here and our jobs have only just begun."

"With love, Bear."

Paws and Reflect

❖ Humans can get lost in the realm of selfish thought. They need to see us and the world as one. ~ Furry

❖ Some animals bring out the best in people, and some animals pay the price for those who never see the light. ~ Furry

❖ I have seen the worst and the best of being in captivity. One can take your spirit away and the other can lift it up. I am thankful for both so that I can truly savor my life now. ~ Kazuma

❖ Humans, in their quest for constant entertainment, miss the magic of just being, of just listening, and experiencing a moment in time. When they rely on outside things for fun, for something spectacular to entertain them, they usually end up disappointed. They go to extreme measures to achieve this level of excitement. Herein lies the basis of their destruction, the foundation is broken. The quality of 'being' is lost. They no longer can hear… from within.   They are hollow vessels, stimulated only by the outside world. ~ Kazuma

❖ Humans have a great capacity to love, animals have a great capacity to forgive. Humans can join together for something they love and miracles happen. I am an example of this. All too often humans think that to love too much shows weakness when in reality it shows great strength.
~ Kazuma

❖ Just like people, animals that show extremes of their personality can be classified as a bit crazy. As long as we know what is acceptable and when to act a certain way, it is not crazy. ~ AnnaBelle

❖ Without forgiveness the heart cannot beat fully and cannot love fully. Forgiveness is essential to experience all that the heart has to offer. It is the essential building block of moving forward in life. ~ AnnaBelle

❖ Stress is pollution. Animals see it, feel it, and know it. You have to find a way to 'mainstream', to focus your attention and let life's other debris be swept away. Stress looks like polluted air floating around a person's energy. It is not a sharp energy with a vibration; instead it is stagnant, heavy and dark. It slows down the flow of good energy, and creates sludge. ~ AnnaBelle

❖ Humans let their minds control their spirit. That's all mixed up! When I see a person who is balanced, they appear to me with a clear energy field, a lovely vibration to it, and soft hues of color mixed through. The body, mind, and spirit are aligned. I know this when I see a light at the top of the head. Not many people appear this way. But there are a few. People need to aspire to this. Less stress pollution will translate into surprising benefits for all. ~ AnnaBelle

❖ No matter what you encounter in this life, you will always have your spirit. When you forget that, you will be finished. Your spirit is the embodiment of your creation, so fan that flame and let it shine bright. ~ Tsunami

❖ We are all connected. What you do to me, you do to you. People need to live with their hearts wide open. They need to hear with their conscience and see with their heart. ~ Zena

❖ I have confidence in my life now. That was not always the case. I come from broken pieces. But what I have found throughout my life is that there is one thing that can mend any broken piece. Even the shattered pieces of our lives can be restored. That remedy is love. ~ Zena

❖ The majesty of my being is the ability to forget my past in order to see myself once again through the heart of a human. It is hard to see your reflection when the heart cannot reflect. ~ Magic

❖ Disease serves many purposes that you may not know. It challenges the very spirit to a war of wills, faith and tolerance. It is one of our greatest lessons here on earth. ~ Indian

❖ People will need to learn to be one with the land and animals in order to survive. The light will shine again, but those who are forced to live without their conveniences will miss the opportunity at this time to evolve. ~ Bubba

❖ God exists in each of us as love. Yet so many don't ever tap into this amazing potential when all we need to do is ask. Find something to howl for, and then use love to accomplish it to the highest extent possible. Love in its purest form is the source of miracles. It is where all else stems from. Fear is where the dark festers. Know this, for it is the rule of the future. ~ Isis

❖ Passing out of a physical body is a surrendering to the great hands of light. When our spirit begins to lift from the body, many try to hold on. However, when it is time, there is nothing that can be done except to surrender to this great force. It is powerful and fast, dizzying to some as you shift into a spiritual realm. Then you begin to feel the immense love infused over you, as if you are weak and limp, yet full of a vibration of love, like no other. ~ Lakota

❖ It is your angels who help you from the body, this I know because I have seen their wings. I have felt hands supporting me as I left my physical body. When you get to the light, the faces of those you have known before come into view. It is like a birth. ~ Lakota

❖ Just a minute of time in spirit would be enough to get in touch again with the understanding of divine love, and connection with all. I share my bed with humans and animals here. There is no competition, no hatred. It is the true garden of love. This is our deepest desire for the earth at this time, to reestablish this harmony among all. ~ Lakota

❖ We know when humans interact with us. We feel their love and pain. They are our hope for survival. ~ Whales

❖ We are wise beyond your comprehension, with wisdom and information hundreds of years deep embedded in our cells. We coordinate healing circles and songs, we mourn death and extend our compassion among ourselves and also out to the humans. We hold high levels of emotions and absorb sound energy through our bodies in a way that decodes and understands every intricate detail. It is a full knowing. ~ Whales

❖ Soon people will begin to experience a dual consciousness. Many already have, and find this world too painful to stay in. This is why many are leaving. As we awaken to this higher level of existence we will become aware of the unity of souls. The earth is really just a reflection of the energy within ourselves, our country, and our world. ~ Whales

❖ People need to rescue that part of them that became detached, that refuses to move forward, that chooses anger, guilt, and resentment as their source of nutrition instead of love. They need to reach in, take the hand of that child inside, and bring them into the light of love and forgiveness. ~ Miss Puss

❖ If we all fixed the broken bridges within us that keep us from the truth or the divine, access to a higher existence would become immediate, palpable and real. Fix the bridges and all that was lost will be found within you. ~ Miss Puss

- ❖ I love the music of life, the symphony when things are in harmony. I love to observe this. ~ Miss Puss

- ❖ Most of you use logic to arrive at a conclusion. Although logic serves a great purpose, if you use it without compassion, grace, and respect, the answer can be dramatically different than what it really should be. ~ Miss Puss

- ❖ What I distinctly remember about shifting out of my body is the feeling of being weightless. I felt as if I was in a hollow tunnel. It seemed to echo. I began thinking about when I was a young cub. I was small and I could see my mother. I was immediately filled with what I can describe as a type of exhilaration and excitement. At that moment everything sparkled and glowed. I felt like a cub as I awoke to a realm of beauty. My mother was there, she licked me and I felt at peace and at home. ~ Tigger

- ❖ Don't people understand that just by treating one being with disrespect and hate creates a blemish and a hole in the soul of existence? ~ Benny

- ❖ People wear many covers, layer upon layer. Underneath all of them is their soul, their true self. I just want them to walk naked, to feel what it is to be free from all layers, diversions, walls, and masks. In this humble state, they will feel like never before. Yes, your species needs to feel once again. ~ Benny

- ❖ One of the things I have learned is that the higher your vibration, the more you can manifest. ~ Benny

- ❖ Some of us are not meant for captivity. We are not wired that way. I think it is quite apparent those who are, and those who aren't. ~ Ranger Fuzzy Bear

❖ Only in knowing weakness first can you truly appreciate the full scope of strength and grace.   What we learn here (earth) will only enhance what you can do over there (spirit). ~ Miss Ollie

❖ The human race has been put in a position over the years to enable a change to occur both personally and globally. This can have dramatic effects if enough people follow through. The animals cling tight to the earth's energy. It is our substance. We all play a vital role in its survival; this is what we are worried about. ~ Gulliver

❖ As we vibrate at a higher frequency we will be able to experience what others feel, to experience their full being, just by intending to feel it. Once we get to this level, we will banish prejudice, racism, and judgment. If we could actually see each being's soul, there would be no hate.
~ Gulliver

❖ Listen to what we have to say. Absorb our ancient knowledge and wisdom. This is the start of being able to live in a world you have only dreamed of. A world where compassion and love rules each being. As the quest for truth unfolds before your eyes, our heart's love will overshadow the negative. It is a divine world, and you are welcome to it.
~ Gulliver

❖ Birds are the greatest diagnostic tool this planet has. Through our actions, migrations and habitat, you can tell a lot about certain areas of this planet.
~ Sierra

❖ We are a species made up of heart and pride, so we work through our pain so that we can continue to please. We may not be as good as we were, but we try hard to do what we once did. We don't wish to disappoint. We work through the pain and suffer silently later.
~Finnegan

❖ People should acknowledge the older animals. They are special in their own way. And just because they may not be able to perform at the level they once did, their jobs can be changed so that their worth and wisdom is never taken for granted or overlooked. ~ Finnegan

❖ Love conquers the darkest soul, the deepest pain and the broken spirit. Open your heart so that the wings of love can fly. ~ Champ

❖ Our deepest desire is to partner with people, to love them, protect them, and have them acknowledge this back. Forgiveness is not something we think about, it just happens. ~ Roxy

❖ I will say that the people who live and care for animals on a deep level begin to think the way we do. They understand things from our viewpoint and when this happens they become a master on the human level. There are animal and human "masters" who rise above ego for the higher purpose of all. ~ Roxy

❖ I do not look to the future and want for anything. I stay in the present. In this state of mind, I can be the best I can be at all times. It is what we think and do in the present that matters. The future depends on this. ~ Roxy

❖ When a heart has loved fully without restraint you will have witnessed what it feels like for a dog to love. We do not hold back. When we love something we love it with our whole being. There is no mid way, or kind of. ~ Roxy

❖ People are the makers and breakers of all we have. We have reason to fear the ones that lose their connection to the soul which connects us all. However, every lost soul can be found, and that is where we come in. The animal world operates behind the scenes silently tugging at people to get back on track. ~ Roxy

Acknowledgements: Debbie McGillivray

My deepest love and thanks to God for allowing me to communicate with the animals so that their messages may be heard.

Love and gratitude to all the animals both alive and in spirit that have graciously contributed to this book and our lives. Your messages will be heard and awareness will be achieved because of you. I am honored to be your voice.

A special thank you to those whose sweat and tears go into making this world a better place for all God's creatures. I have had the pleasure of meeting many amazing people who give of themselves unselfishly every day to create sanctuaries for the many animals in need. Thank you Laurie Coren at Octagon Wildlife Refuge, Debbie Cobb at Suncoast Primates, Suzie Williams at Joshua's Haven, and the many others who are earth angels to the animals, thank you!

For the creation of this book, *Untamed Voices, Volume 1*, I want to especially thank my co-author, Sue Steffens for being the fuel for this fire. Without her this idea may still be just that. She will jump any hurdle to bring about a better world for all the animals on this planet. Her dedication to the animals is unconditional. She is an inspiration.

Thank you to Wilbur McCauley for holding down the fort at Tigers for Tomorrow, while we pursue this venture. I am grateful for your unwavering dedication to the welfare of animals globally and of course your kind and compassionate "lion heart."

Thank you to David Cummings for seeing our vision while editing and preparing this book for print. Your time and dedication is so appreciated.

To our crew of photographers, thank you for capturing the true essence of these magnificent beings

A lifetime of thanks to my master teachers, my horse Finnegan, who put me on my path, Jimmy James Junior who taught me about the love of souls, and Champ who taught me about forgiveness and joy.

My sons, who are a gift from God and fill my heart with the deepest love. I hope to expose you to the magnificent messages from the animals so that one day you can set the example for your generation and bring about awareness for the sake of the planet and its creatures.

To my loving parents for teaching me at a very young age the importance of respect for all life and for supporting the work I do with enthusiasm and pride. And finally to my husband, Scott, thank you for your love and support throughout this process and for inspiring me to be the best I can. Thank you for making me laugh when I need it most. I love you.

Acknowledgements: Sue Steffens

I give thanks to my creator who has granted me such a wonderful life filled with great beings, humans and animals of so many varieties. My heart belongs to the animals that I have shared this world with. The animals found me when I was lost, and they have given strength when I needed to be strong. Tawny and Cosmo are the two tigers that were the first to teach me that animals are so much more than what we see; they are intelligent, kind, smart, they have intellect and emotions, likes and dislikes and mostly how deep they can love us back. They were the catalyst that inspired the founding of Tigers For Tomorrow.

My two wolf hybrids, Amstel and Dakota, who taught me to live in the moment, and Bear and Lakota, my first two Gray wolves who are my guides and angels.

For giving me the opportunity to be involved in such an incredible book, I thank my friend, Debbie McGillivray. She has given unconditionally to the preserve for many years and I am honored to be a part of something that will change the way many people view animals. Debbie is one of the most real and down-to-earth people I have been graced with meeting in this life. Thank you for being my friend and a friend to all the animals we share our planet with.

My dearest friends, Robert Lumino, Anthony and Suzanne Sparta, Greg Faherty, Jurgen Krause, Lisa Ann Dimarsico, Karen Fagen and Joe Alexander, who, when I left New York assured me I could always come home. Untamed Mountain has become my home now, yet each one of these very special people gave me support and courage to go out and follow my dreams and they each will always have a very special place in my heart.

I am lucky to work with three exceptional human beings, Andy Daugherty, Sandy Johnson and Tia Gaines. These three keepers keep the preserve running and all of our animals happy and that means the world to me. With all my heart thank you.

Thank you to my mother who always encouraged my dreams and my step mother Lois, who picked up where my father left off.

To the person who has helped me most become the person who I am today and who has given his heart and soul to make my dreams come true, my husband Wilbur McCauley. Wilbur has given me his unconditional support and love – even at times when I may not have deserved it. He has never been jealous of the other male in my life, "Benny the black Leopard." He has stood by me and the animals through the storms, the rebuilding, the moving, the expansion, the losses and sadness, with unwavering strength and love. He has the heart of a lion, thank you dearheart.

Photographer Credits

A very special thank you to our crew of photographers who captured the personality and essence of the animals featured in this book.

David Cummings: Cover: (Kazuma), page 66 (Willow), page 71 (Ravi), page 78 (Sam)

Lesa Cummings: page 24 (Valkeri), page 41 (Towzer), page 42 (Ellie), Page 70 (Boris), page 80 (Aurora and Sam)

E.S. Cummingham: page 97 (Brother)

Lisa Ann Dimarsico Smith: page 13 (Roxy & Sue)

Sandy Johnson: page III (Sue & Kalel), page 73 (Tawny), page III (Dakota-Cougar), page 12 (Benny), page 18 (Furry), page 19 (Lakota), page 21 (Orion), page 24 (Valhala), page 25 (Ms. Puss), page 31 (Harley), page 36 (Ayla), page 55 & 56 (Mr. Lion), page 60 (Tsunami), page 61 (Pepper), page 62 (Magic), page 65 (Katie), page 69 (Boris), page 71(Ravi), page 73 (Tawny), page 77 (Yonah), page 83 (Mojo), page 85 (Rudy), page 89 (Miss Ollie), page 87 (Herk& Zena), page 91 (Lt. Ranger Fuzzy Bear), page 92 (Fuzz & Cody), page 95 (Isis)

Larry G. Kinney: Wildlife Photographer - InOurSight.com & larrygkinney.com: page 5 (Deb and Ayla), page 9 (Benny), page 17 (Furry), page 33 (Annabelle), page 59 (Tsunami)

Donald J. Knapp: page 39 (Luke), page 67 & 68 (Lilly), page 79 (Deb, Sue & Sam)

Michael Korbert: page 63 (Spike)

Ray Malin: page 105 (Bear Wolf)

Jake McGillivray: page 49 (Finnegan), page 50 (Finnegan and Deb), page 101 & 104 (whales)

Creedon McGillivray: Page 29 & 30 (Mirabella)

Kiska Moore: page 51 (Artimis), page 57 (Bubba), page 81 (Sierra)

Ron Priest: page 74 (Pongo), page 75 (Pongo), page 92 (Cheetah), page 117 (Debbie Cob and Chimp)

Sue Steffens: page 45 (Tigger)

April White: page 28 (Barney), page 58 (Grumpy), page 119 (Susan Williams & cub)

Tracy Williams: page 118 (Lauri and Ally)

Many of the animals featured in this book reside at sanctuaries and preserves where they will live out the remainder of their lives. These facilities dedicate their lives to giving the animals in their care love and respect. Featured below are three of the sanctuaries we visited.

Suncoast Primate Sanctuary: Palm Harbor, FL

Alternate Highway 19
Palm Harbor, Florida 34683
Contact Us at 727-943-5897

Suncoast Primate Sanctuary is not only a sanctuary for the animals, but for people also. Suncoast is a 501-c3 nonprofit primate sanctuary that has the largest animal, children and senior programs in Pinellas County Florida. Suncoast Primate Sanctuary believes that no animal, child or senior should be left behind because of money. Everyone needs help in life and often it begins with the community. Suncoast Primate Sanctuary has been in Palm Harbor Florida for 62 years. They provide homes mainly for primates many of which come from research labs, Zoos and sometimes private owners. Some well known animals such as Otto from American Tourist, Pongo from Mazda, and Cheetah from Tarzan have resided here. They have some of the oldest living animals in the world.

Debbie Cobb is fifty three and a fifth generation family working with animals. Her greatest loves are God and family both human and non human. Her husband is her best friend and they are proud parents of twin girls, who also love the animals. Debbie Cobb has worked and played with approximately 150 Chimps, 30 Orangutans, and 30 Gorillas. She believes that one person can make a difference. "It is not what you do in life; it is what you leave that makes a difference. Stay positive and be the good in everyday."

Please visit them in person or online at www.suncoastprimate.org
Hours: Mon – Wed: Closed
Thu – Sun: 10am – 4pm

Octagon Wildlife Sanctuary: Punta Gorda, FL

41660 Horseshoe Road, Punta Gorda, FL 33982,
(239) 543-1130 -Hours: Sat & Sun 11a.m. - 4 p.m

Octagon Wildlife Sanctuary, a 501-c3 nonprofit, was founded approximately 34 years ago when two bears from "the Gentle Ben" series were found by Fish and Wildlife Control. They were left in a broken down trailer to die. FWC, not knowing what to do with them stopped at a nearby fire station. Firemen Peter Caron and his father Omer had just bought 10 acres of land down the road and volunteered to safely house the bears. They built an enclosure for the bears in a couple of days and when it was done they coaxed the bears out of the container with a blueberry pie and into the enclosure. This was the beginning of the sanctuary known as "Octagon." From that day, Octagon became a home for all of the abused, neglected and mistreated animals that Fish and Wildlife or the USDA confiscate. Octagon has made a safe haven for many animals throughout the U.S. Once they accept an animal they keep it for the rest of that animal's life. Octagon believes that the animal needs to know that it will be safe, happy and treated with love and respect for the rest of their life. They have approximately 120 animals that are housed on over 10 acres in south Punta Gorda, Florida. "We try to educate each and everyone that visits our sanctuary about each animal's unique story."

Omer Caron passed away in 1983 and Peter Caron passed away in 2005. Peter's wife, Lauri, stepped in after Pete's passing and still to this day is committed to the daily running of the sanctuary. Lauri Caron was originally from Rockford, Illinois. When Lauri was a little kid, she wanted to own her own kennel. She states, "Little did I know how this would become a reality with animals much bigger than domestic dogs and cats!" Lauri heard about Octagon at a church she was attending. When she finally moved to Florida in 1993, she was in search of this amazing place she heard about called Octagon. It took her three weeks to find it and when she did she never looked back. Lauri majored in Biology in college, but was never prepared for what she was about to spend her whole life in doing. When she has time to get away, she enjoys going to the beach, watching movies, listening to area bands, or riding her Harley!

Please visit Octagon in person or online at www.octagonwildlife.org

Joshua's Haven: Plant City, FL

Just a tid bit about me, Susan Williams. I was born and raised in rural Florida. Growing up we always had the typical animals such as dogs, cats and farm stock. In 2007 my brother became ill and needed care. I moved to Alabama to help him and to seek further treatment for his condition. Sadly, he eventually passed from cancer. While caring for my brother, I reconnected with an old friend who was now a Doctor and also operated a wild animal park.

Now you should know that prior to 2007 I had never been to a circus, pet store or zoo. I didn't like the thought of seeing animals in cages. To my surprise the Doctor needed help running the animal park. I became involved thinking it would only be temporary. It was a rude awakening to come to the realization that these animals would never return to the land that their species originated from. They are captive bred and born, human imprinted animals. They are not 'wild' in the sense that they cannot fend and care for themselves; however they always have their instincts and that's what makes them dangerous. The animal park became the most important part of my life. I grew to love these animals in a way I never knew was possible. Many years later, and through much soul searching, I decided to open my own private sanctuary for exotic animals who needed a forever home. That was the birth of Joshua's Haven.

Joshua's Haven is a peaceful place where the animals can live out their last years with no exhibiting or breeding. I spend my days caring, loving, playing, talking and enriching their lives. They will never want or need for anything. The only way for people to love, care and want to save these magnificent creatures is to learn about them. I believe that wildlife educators and ambassador animals play a crucial role in the plight of extinction. Throughout the years of meeting many animal people and visiting different facilities, I was able to witness my first animal reading of a black bear I helped care for. I was shocked to hear the things the communicator said. No one knew I sneaked him popsicles, yet the woman told me that's what the bear said. It was as if he was speaking directly to me. In this industry you never ever know everything. The animals have opened my heart and I have learned to keep my mind open. It's a constant learning and a changing way of life. Beliefs are as vast as the species we care for. I am open and willing to learn from all.

53676519R00074

Made in the USA
Lexington, KY
14 July 2016